CLARE LATIMER

The Comfort Food Cookbook

PRION

Paperback edition published 1998 by
Prion Books Ltd.,
32-34 Gordon House Road,
London NW5 1LP

First published 1996

A catalogue record of this book can be obtained from the British Library.

ISBN 1-85375-288-6

Cover design by Bob Eames
Interior artwork by Joanna Venus

Printed and bound in Singapore
by Kyodo Printing Pte

To Zoë and Lauren

Contents

Introduction

Soups

Sandwiches

Savoury Snacks

Egg Dishes

Smoked Cod and Sweetcorn Soufflé *48*
Cheese and Bacon Soufflé *49*
Mediterranean Soufflé *50*

Main Course Dishes

Scallops in Ginger Wine *55*
Corned Beef Hash *56*
Cauliflower Cheese *57*
Mixed Cheese Fondue *58*
Stuffed Marrow *59*
Multi-Storey Pizza *60*
Chicken Satay with Sauce *62*
Pesto Gnocchi with Sun-Dried Tomatoes *63*
Skate Wings with Lemon Butter *64*
Roti with Spicy Beef *65*
Roast Chicken with Black Pudding Stuffing
and Bread Sauce *66*
Shepherd's Pie *68*
Steak and Kidney Pudding *70*
Roquefort and Leek Quiche *71*
Madame Bubble and Squeak *72*
Roast Rib of Beef with Yorkshire Pudding *73*
Pot Au Feu *74*
Fish Cakes with Dill Sauce *75*
Kedgeree *76*

Puddings

Sweet Snacks

Comfort Drinks

Index

Introduction

With this big, tough world creating havoc all around us, comfort food is becoming more and more an essential part of our lives. Thankfully, the invasion of nouvelle cuisine, where the portions were delicate in flavour, very rich in substance and only enough to feed a sparrow, has lead to a more sensible way of eating: larger portions than nouvelle cuisine but smaller than the American-sized platefuls we used to attack.

I think it's very important to satisfy your cravings as soon as they strike. I have always allowed myself to eat butter and full fat milk and believe eating the things I want in moderation makes me eat less in the long run. When I attempt to resist temptation and stick to a good healthy salad I often find myself picking at other things for the rest of the evening and end up eating more than if I'd had a reasonable helping of something really comforting.

So what is comfort food? Everyone recognises comfort food when they see it, even if they've never heard the term before. Whether as a cure for a bleak winter's night, or a hot and stressful day at work, comfort food is the gratifying culinary indulgence we reach for when we need to cheer ourselves or our loved-ones up. To me, it includes small treats that are easily accessible: sticky chocolate biscuits hiding in a tin or savoury cheese straws. Another important aspect is simple, relaxing cooking. which is very therapeutic and can reduce stress. The final and most important aspect is to take you back to childhood when life was safe, cosy and surrounded by love. This is the area at which I have aimed hardest in this book. I have used nursery ideas, but then added a few up-to-date ingredients, which are optional, to turn the recipes into the type of dishes being served in many top restaurants.

  Tuck into this book and you will find a cosy comfort world starting to envelop you. Good luck.

Clare Latimer

Soups

Basic Chicken Stock

This stock will do for any of the following soups that require stock and, if you are feeling poorly, it makes a very good comfort drink with lots of goodness. Whenever you have a used chicken carcass, make this stock then keep it in the freezer for a soup-making day.

1 chicken carcass
1 onion, quartered
2 carrots, peeled and cut into large pieces
1 stick celery, washed and cut into large pieces

1 leek, washed and cut into large pieces
1 bouquet garni or mixed fresh herbs
Salt and freshly ground black pepper

Put all the ingredients in a large saucepan, add water to cover and bring to the boil. Cover, then simmer for 1 hour, topping up with water if necessary. Leave to cool and then strain. Remove the fat from the top with a spoon. Store in the fridge for a few days or freeze until ready to use.

Tomato, Lemon Grass and Pesto Soup

SERVES 4

This soup is quick to make and has a subtle taste of lemon grass pervading the pesto aroma. Serve with hot garlic bread if possible. Vegetable stock is easy to make, so I have given you the recipe, but if you are pushed for time then buy some ready-made stock.

For the stock:
1 tbsp olive oil
1 small onion, cut into quarters
Handful onion skins
Handful carrot peelings
Handful cleaned potato peelings
Few stalks celery, roughly chopped
Bunch mixed herbs, such as parsley, sage, thyme, mint, coriander
4 bay leaves
1 litre (1¾ pints) water
Salt and freshly ground black pepper

For the soup:
700g (1½ lb) tomatoes
1 stick lemon grass, finely chopped
Juice of 1 lemon
1 desp caster sugar
1 desp pesto sauce
1 desp tomato purée
1 desp black olive paste – optional
8 large prawns, shelled – optional

Put all the stock ingredients into a heavy-based saucepan, bring to the boil, cover and simmer for 1 hour adding more water if necessary. Strain and put the stock back in the pan. Discard the flavourings.

To make the soup, score the tomato skins and then plunge them into boiling water.

Leave for 1 minute, rinse in cold water and then peel. Halve and then remove the seeds with your hands. Put the tomatoes and all the remaining ingredients except the prawns into the stock and simmer for 10 minutes. Liquidize, add the prawns, make up to 1.2 litres (2 pints) with water, reheat and serve hot.

Pea and Bacon Soup

SERVES **4**

*If you do not have time to make chicken stock,
you can buy ready-made stock or use a stock cube but, if you do,
reduce the amount of salt in the soup as stock cubes are quite salty.
Fresh peas have more flavour than frozen so try and make time in
the summer to pod your own.*

1 tbsp olive oil
3 rashers streaky bacon, rind removed and
 finely chopped
1 onion, peeled and chopped
1 litre (1¾ pints) chicken stock –
 see page 3

Salt and freshly ground black pepper
900g (2lbs) peas
Handful fresh mint, chopped
1 tsp sugar

Heat the oil in a large saucepan and add the bacon. Cook gently for a few minutes to release the fat. Add the onion and cook slowly for 5 minutes. Add the stock, salt, pepper and peas and bring to the boil. Cover and simmer for 20 minutes. Add the mint and sugar and cook for a further 10 minutes. Pour into a liquidizer and whizz on high until smooth. Serve hot.

Barley Soup

SERVES **4**

---

*This is a wonderful meal-type soup great for
a cold winter's night.*

1 tbsp olive oil
1 carrot, peeled and finely diced
2 tender sticks celery, washed and finely
   diced
1 large potato, peeled and diced
1 small leek, washed and diced
¼ Savoy cabbage, washed and finely
   shredded
½ onion, peeled and studded with 6 cloves

120g (4oz) pearl barley
4 rashers streaky bacon, rind removed and
   finely chopped
Salt and freshly ground black pepper
1 litre (1¾ pints) chicken stock
1 egg yolk
150ml (¼ pint) double cream
1 tbsp parsley, finely chopped

Put the oil in a large saucepan and then add all the vegetables, barley, bacon and seasoning. Sweat over a medium heat for a few minutes and then add the chicken stock. Cover and simmer slowly for one hour. Check the seasoning, mix the egg yolk and cream in a small bowl or cup then pour the mixture into the soup. Ladle into serving bowls, sprinkle with the parsley and serve.

Borscht

SERVES 6

---

*Beetroot is not the most popular vegetable but part of the problem
is that people shy away before trying it. I have cooked this
soup many times for dinner parties and the bowls
have always been cleaned out.*

I tbsp oil
I onion, peeled and finely chopped
450g (I lb) raw beetroot, peeled and finely
   chopped or grated
I large carrot, peeled and chopped
I stick tender celery, washed and finely
   chopped

700g (I ½ lbs) lean beef bones – optional
I.4 litres (2½ pints) water
Salt and freshly ground black pepper
I desp caster sugar
Juice of 2 lemons
I 50ml (¼ pint) soured cream
Small handful chives, chopped

Put the oil in a heavy-based saucepan, add the prepared vegetables, sweat for a few minutes then add the beef bones, water and seasoning. Bring to the boil, cover, then simmer for 45 minutes. Remove the bones and liquidize the soup, then pour it back into the saucepan. Add the sugar and lemon juice and adjust the seasoning. Serve hot or cold garnished with a dollop of soured cream in each bowl and sprinkled with the chives.

Mixed Bean Soup

SERVES 2

This is a lovely thick, soothing and delicious soup. When great friends of mine had a tragedy recently, I took round a tub of this soup and it certainly helped console them. The Parmesan can be 'shaved' with a peeler.

I tbsp oil
I large red onion, peeled and chopped
I clove garlic, peeled and crushed
I stick celery, washed and chopped
225g (8oz) French beans, topped, tailed and chopped
225g (8oz) broad beans, podded

I litre (1¾ pints) chicken stock – see page 3
Salt and freshly ground black pepper
Small handful fresh basil, finely chopped
2 tbsp virgin olive oil
25g (1oz) Parmesan cheese, shaved

Heat the oil in a large saucepan and add the onion and garlic. Cook slowly for five minutes until soft but not browning. Add the celery, beans, chicken stock, salt and pepper and bring to the boil. Reduce the heat, cover and simmer for 30 minutes. Pour into a liquidizer and whizz until smooth. Check the seasoning and add the basil. Stir well, then pour into serving bowls. Drizzle the olive oil over the top and garnish with the Parmesan shavings. Serve hot.

Dark Onion Soup

SERVES 3

The best answer for a cold: the aroma of onion helps to clear the head and there are lots of vitamins to help recovery. Even if you do not have a cold, it makes a very good supper dish to warm the cockles. Add a dash of brandy to spark it up.

450g (1lb) onions, peeled and thinly sliced
1 clove garlic, peeled and crushed
1 tbsp olive oil
25g (1oz) butter
1 level tsp caster sugar

1 litre (1¾ pints) chicken stock
 – see page 3
Salt and freshly ground black pepper
120g (4oz) Gruyère cheese, grated
4 slices French bread
Freshly grated nutmeg

Put the onion, garlic, oil, butter and sugar in a large heavy-based saucepan and cook gently for 5 minutes or until soft and lightly browned. Add the stock and season with the salt and pepper. Bring to the boil and simmer for 1 hour. Preheat the grill to high. Divide the cheese into four and press firmly onto one side of each slice of bread. Grill until the cheese is melted and lightly browned. Pour the soup into serving dishes and press a cheese toasty well down into each bowl so that the bread soaks up the juices. Top with a little freshly grated nutmeg and serve hot.

9

Sandwiches

Sandwiches

Sandwiches are not only a very good quick snack, but can be very soothing on a hectic or bad day. The varieties of possible fillings are endless but here are a few of my favourites. The quantities are for two sandwiches, so allow four pieces of bread, choosing either a soft, nutty brown slice or crusty light white. I always use butter. One of the quick spreads will do if you prefer, but for me there's no comparison.

Carrot and Cheese

I carrot, peeled and grated
25g (1oz) Cheddar cheese, grated
1 heaped tsp mayonnaise

Salt and freshly ground black pepper
1 tsp finely chopped parsley
4 slices bread

Mix all the ingredients together then spread the mixture on two of the bread slices. Top with the other pieces of bread, cut into four triangles and serve.

Banana, Cream Cheese and Honey

————————

1 banana, peeled and sliced
Squeeze of lemon juice
4 slices bread

50g (2oz) cream cheese
1 desp runny honey

Put the banana slices into a cup with the lemon juice and stir gently until evenly coated. Spread two pieces of bread with the cream cheese and top with the banana.

Spread the remaining pieces of bread with the honey. Sandwich together, cut into four triangles and serve.

Crab and Avocado

————————

1 fresh crab, white and brown flesh
  reserved
1 desp crème fraîche
Salt and freshly ground black pepper
Few drops Tabasco

1 avocado, halved, stone removed, sliced
  and scooped out with a spoon
Juice of ½ lemon
4 slices bread

Mix the crab, crème fraîche, salt, pepper and Tabasco in a cup. Coat the avocado slices with the lemon juice. Spread the crab on the bread and top with the sliced avocado. Sandwich with the other pieces of bread, cut into quarters and serve.

Bacon and Marmalade

---

4 rashers back bacon, rind removed
4 slices bread

50g (2oz) cream cheese
I desp marmalade

Grill the bacon rashers until crisp and brown. Place on two pieces of bread. Spread the other two slices of bread with the cream cheese and marmalade then sandwich together and serve.

Stilton and Redcurrant Jelly

50g (2oz) creamy Stilton cheese, rind
   removed, sliced

4 slices bread
I desp redcurrant jelly

Lay the slices of Stilton on two pieces of bread. Spread the other two pieces of bread with the redcurrant jelly then sandwich together and serve.

Hot Taleggio Sandwich

---

2 soft white baps, halved
Butter for spreading
50g (2oz) Taleggio cheese, sliced
1 tomato, sliced

2 slices ham – optional
Freshly ground black pepper
1 tsp pesto sauce

Preheat the oven to 180°C (350°F, Gas 4). Spread the baps with some butter. On the bottom halves, lay on the Taleggio, tomato slices, the ham if using, and then grind over some pepper. Spread the top halves of the baps with pesto and sandwich together. Wrap in foil and cook in the oven for 15 minutes or until the cheese is runny. Serve immediately.

Hot Croissant with Smoked Chicken, Avocado and Tomato

2 croissants, halved lengthways
1 smoked chicken breast, sliced
1 avocado, halved, stone removed and
  scooped out with spoon

1 tomato, sliced
Freshly ground black pepper
1 tsp jalapeno sauce – optional

Preheat the oven to 200°C (400°F, Gas 6). Take the bottom halves of the croissants and top with the pieces of chicken breast. Arrange the avocado and tomato slices on top then grind over some pepper. Sprinkle the jalapeno sauce on the top half of the croissants and sandwich together. Place on a baking tray and cook in the oven for 5 minutes or until the chicken is warmed through and the croissants are crisp. Serve immediately.

Fried Mozzarella Sandwiches

SERVES 2

Very naughty but very, very nice! Serve with a tomato salad and the naughtiness goes away a little.

4 slices white bread, crusts removed
1 x 125g bag Mozzarella, drained and
   sliced
Fresh basil leaves
Salt and freshly ground black pepper

Black olive paste, for spreading
2 tbsp milk
2 eggs
Olive oil for frying

Lay out two slices of bread and top with the sliced Mozzarella. Scatter with the fresh basil leaves and season with salt and pepper. Spread the other two slices of bread with the black olive paste, spreading right to the edges, and sandwich together. Beat the milk and eggs together in a wide bowl and soak the sandwiches in the liquid for 1 minute. Turn over and repeat. Press the edges of the sandwiches firmly together. Heat the oil in a large frying pan and fry the sandwiches on both sides until golden brown. Drain on kitchen paper and serve immediately.

Savoury Snacks

Vegetable Crisps

Twenty years ago I went to Colorado, USA and had my first deep-fried vegetables. My plan was to rush back to England and market them. Nothing happened! Now there are a few companies who sell bags of delicious mixed vegetable crisps but they are fearfully expensive, so here is a chance to make your own.

I sweet potato, scrubbed
I large raw beetroot, peeled
2 carrots, peeled

I medium parsnip, peeled
I plantain, peeled
Oil for deep-fat frying

Slice all the vegetables wafer-thin using either a slicer or a potato peeler then pat dry with kitchen paper. Heat the oil to 190°C (375°F) and then fry each vegetable separately until crisp and lightly golden. Remove from the fat and drain on kitchen paper. Sprinkle with salt and serve with drinks or a game dish.

Vegetable Pasties

Pasties are a great thing to make when you have the time and then keep in the freezer. Freeze them at the stage when the pasties are made up but not cooked. They can then be taken from frozen, brushed with egg and cooked for 45 minutes at 180°C (350°F, Gas 4). This slower time and temperature will allow for thawing.

For the pastry:
225g (8oz) plain flour
Pinch salt
1 desp Parmesan cheese, finely grated
¼ tsp mustard powder
1 tsp pesto sauce
85g (3oz) butter
Water to mix

For the filling:
1 onion, peeled and finely chopped
1 tbsp oil
1 carrot, peeled and finely diced
6 button mushrooms, wiped and sliced
120g (4oz) swede, peeled and finely chopped
1 courgette, finely chopped
1 small sweet potato, peeled and finely chopped
Handful of parsley, finely chopped
85g (3oz) Gorgonzola cheese, finely diced
1 tbsp crème fraîche
1 tsp tomato purée
Salt and freshly ground black pepper

Preheat the oven to 200°C (400°F, Gas 6). Put the onion and oil in a large frying pan and cook slowly until soft but not brown. Add the rest of the vegetables and cook for a further ten minutes over a low heat. Add the parsley, cheese, crème fraîche, tomato purée and season well.

To make the pastry, put the flour, salt,

Parmesan and mustard into a bowl and mix well. Add the pesto and butter and, using your fingertips, rub until the mixture resembles breadcrumbs. Using a round bladed knife, stir in just enough water to make a stiff dough. Divide into four and roll out each piece on a floured surface to 6mm (¼ in) thick. Place a 20cm (8 in) plate on top of one pastry square to use as a template and cut round it. Repeat with the remaining pastry. Spoon the vegetable mixture into the middle of each pastry circle, wet the edges with water, then fold over and press the edges together firmly, crimping to seal. Carefully place the pasties on a baking tray, brush with beaten egg and cook in the oven for 25 minutes or until the pastry is golden brown. Serve hot.

Freezer friendly

Waffles with Bacon and Maple Syrup

SERVES 2

The Americans certainly know how to comfort themselves with food. Not being terribly concerned about convention, they will combine any flavours, sweet or savoury. Here is the ultimate combination — and for breakfast too !

4 rashers back bacon
2 waffles

Butter for spreading
2 tbsp maple syrup

Preheat the grill to high. Grill the bacon until crisp but not dry. Add the waffles and toast on both sides until crisp. Spread the waffles with a little butter and put on to warmed plates. Spoon over the maple syrup and lay the bacon on the side. Serve hot.

Bacon Röstis

Röstis can be served as a potato dish with a main course, as a starter dish with various toppings or just as little snackets.

450g (1 lb) potatoes, peeled, coarsely grated
  and dried with kitchen paper
Freshly grated nutmeg
Salt and freshly ground black pepper
1 tsp horseradish sauce

1 tsp thyme, finely chopped – optional
4 rashers streaky bacon, rind removed and
  finely chopped
1 tbsp oil

In a bowl, mix the potatoes, nutmeg, salt, pepper, horseradish and thyme. Put the bacon and oil in a large heavy-based frying pan and cook until crisp and brown. Leaving the fat in the pan, remove the bacon pieces and stir them into the potato mix.

For main course röstis, divide the mixture into eight using your hands. Roll each portion into a ball and then flatten. For a starter or snack make about 16 pieces. Fry the röstis, as many as will fit, in the bacon fat for about 5 minutes on each side or until golden brown. For a main course accompaniment, serve at this stage. For a starter, top the röstis with warmed smoked eel fillet and soured cream, or smoked salmon and poached quail eggs, or experiment with your own ideas.

Cheese Straws

MAKES ABOUT **40** STRAWS

These are very useful things to keep to hand in a tin to serve either as a quick comfort snack or with drinks if friends drop round. The pastry is also very good for making little biscuits to spread with cream cheese and smoked salmon.

120g (4oz) plain flour
Pinch salt
Pinch mustard powder
Pinch paprika
50g (2oz) butter

50g (2oz) Cheddar cheese, grated
1 egg yolk
Water, to mix
1 egg mixed with 2 tsp milk for glaze

Preheat the oven to 200°C (400°F, Gas 6). Mix the flour, salt, mustard and paprika in a bowl. Cut in the butter and, using your fingertips, rub until it resembles fine breadcrumbs. Stir in the cheese and egg yolk with a round bladed knife and then add just enough water to make a stiff dough. Roll out the pastry on a floured surface to a thickness of 5mm (¼in). Cut into thin straws about 7.5cm (3in) long and then place on a greased baking tray, twisting each straw into a spiral if you wish. Brush with the egg and milk mixture and bake for 10 – 15 minutes or until pale golden. Cool and then store in a tin.

Croque Monsieur

SERVES 2

---

*A French version of the Mozzarella sandwich,
but not good for vegetarians.
If you want to make it more of a meal, fry some rashers of
back bacon, grill some tomato halves and serve with a
fried egg on the sandwich.*

25g (1oz) butter
4 slices white bread
4 slices ham

120g (4oz) Gruyère cheese, grated
Mustard for spreading – optional
Oil for frying

Butter the bread and top two of the slices with a slice of ham and then the cheese. Spread the remaining pieces of bread with mustard, if using, and sandwich together.

Heat the oil in a large frying pan and fry the sandwiches on both sides until golden brown. Serve hot.

Chicken Livers on Toast

SERVES 2

This is a great supper dish — very quick and easy to make. The booze is optional but very comforting on a cold winter night. I have suggested using fresh herbs but you can use dried if needs must. Serve with a salad.

25g (1oz) butter
1 clove garlic, peeled and crushed — optional
225g (8oz) chicken livers
Sprigs of thyme, oregano and sage, freshly chopped

Splash cooking brandy
Splash port
2 slices bread, brown or white, crusts removed
Butter for spreading

Put the butter and garlic in a large frying pan and cook gently for 2 minutes. Add the chicken livers and herbs and cook for another 2 minutes or so, stirring occasionally. Add the brandy and port, set light to the pan — watching your eyebrows — and cook for as long as you wish. You can serve the livers pink or well done. Toast the bread, spread with butter, put on serving plates and spoon on the livers. Serve hot.

Battered Vegetables

SERVES 4 – 8

I was at a wedding recently and these were served with the champagne as a canapé. They would be equally good to munch by an open fire, in front of the telly or in the garden on a summer day. Deep-fried food is always delicious and, with vegetables, it is not too naughty. The tomato dip adds freshness and, if you are a heat fan, just add a few extra drops of Tabasco. If you prefer, they can be fried in advance and then reheated in a hot oven (200°C, 400°F, Gas 6) for about 10 minutes. This helps remove any excess fat, the vegetables taste just as good, if not better — and it's certainly better for the waistline!

Handful each of some of the following:
  bite-sized chunks of red pepper,
  courgettes, aubergine, cauliflower florets,
  green or purple sprouting broccoli florets,
  asparagus tips, red onions, sweet
  potatoes, parsley sprigs, chive or
  courgette flowers

For the batter:
175g (6oz) plain flour
Pinch salt
1 desp Parmesan cheese, finely grated –
  optional

200ml (⅓ pint) water
Vegetable oil for frying

For the tomato dip:
1 desp olive oil
1 red onion, peeled and roughly chopped
1 clove garlic, peeled and crushed
4 tomatoes, peeled, deseeded and roughly
  chopped
½tsp sugar
Salt and freshly ground black pepper
3 drops Tabasco
Small handful coriander – optional

Put the flour, salt, Parmesan and water into a liquidizer and process for 30 seconds. Leave to stand. Heat the oil in a deep-fryer to 190˚C (375˚F). (If you do not have a thermometer then drop in a crumb of bread, which should sizzle straight away when the oil is hot enough.) Dip the vegetables into the batter and then deep-fry for about 3 — 4 minutes or 1 minute for the parsley, chive or courgette flowers. The batter should be golden brown and the vegetables cooked. Drain on kitchen paper and serve hot.

To make the tomato dip, put the olive oil, onion and garlic into a saucepan and cook gently for five minutes or until the onion is soft but not browning.   Add the tomatoes, sugar, salt, pepper and Tabasco and stir well. Gently cook for a further five minutes. Put the mixture into a liquidizer with the coriander and process on high for a few seconds. Pour into a serving bowl, place on a large plate and surround with the cooked vegetables.

Dips with Crudités

————————

*These are great for a light lunch, drinks party or an evening
snack and are very healthy and satisfying. Choose one of the
following dips and chop up any of the crudités suggested.
The dips could also be served instead of the tomato sauce with the
battered vegetables on page 31.*

Crudités

————————

Cauliflower, cut into small florets
Carrots, peeled and cut into fingers
Cucumber, cut into fingers
Radishes, trimmed
Cherry tomatoes, stalks removed

Red peppers, decored, deseeded and cut
  into strips
Young courgettes, cut into fingers
Button mushrooms, halved and stalks
  removed

Warm Cheese Dip

———————

1 tbsp olive oil
1 medium onion, peeled and finely chopped
150ml (¼ pint) double cream
120g (4oz) Red Leicester cheese, grated

1 tsp jalapeno sauce or a few drops
 Tabasco
Freshly ground black pepper
Freshly grated nutmeg

Heat the oil in a frying pan and add the onion. Cook gently for 5 minutes or until soft but not browning. Pour the onion mixture into a liquidizer and process until smooth. Add the cream and process for a few seconds more then pour into a saucepan. Add the cheese and stir over a low heat until the cheese has melted. Add the jalapeno sauce or Tabasco, pepper and nutmeg and pour into a warmed bowl.

Quick and Creamy Dip

———————

1 red onion, grated
Handful fresh mint, finely chopped

150ml (¼ pint) crème fraîche

Mix all the ingredients together and put into a bowl. Serve chilled.

Snack Attack

This is definitely the worst recipe for health in this book, but remember that the theme is comfort, and this is where it comes into its own. Dipped into apple sauce (see page 93), the pork crackling can be served with drinks or just eaten in front of the telly. If you can find a decent butcher — a rare thing these days — ask for a piece of rind from the loin of pork.

1 piece pork skin
Salt

Preheat the oven to 200°C (400°F, Gas 6). Score the pork skin well and rub salt all over it. Place on a baking sheet and cook for about 45 minutes or until golden brown, bubbling and very crunchy. Break up into pieces and enjoy with apple sauce.

Warmed Smoked Eel with Horseradish Sauce

SERVES 4

A friend brought back a whole smoked eel from Amsterdam recently and was told the best way to remove the bones was to warm it through. We put it in the oven for a few minutes and it worked beautifully — the flavour improved to perfection as well. As smoked eel is quite rich, it is best served with a sharp invigorating sauce and chunks of brown bread.

I whole smoked eel, approximately 680g
  (1½lbs)
I desp horseradish sauce
150ml (¼ pint) double cream, whipped
4 handfuls mixed leaves, such as rocket,

oakleaf, lamb's lettuce
8 cherry tomatoes, halved
I tbsp olive oil
I desp balsamic vinegar
Rock salt and freshly ground black pepper

Preheat the oven to 150°C (300°F, Gas 2). Place the eel on a baking tray and warm it in oven for 10 minutes. Meanwhile, fold the horseradish sauce into the whipped cream. Put a handful of salad leaves on each serving plate, garnish with the cherry tomatoes, drizzle over the olive oil and the vinegar and season with salt and pepper. Take the warmed eel from the oven, remove the skin and bones and slice it into manageable pieces. Place the fillets evenly over the dressed salad and serve.

Caramelized Jerusalem Artichokes with Sour Cream

SERVES 4

Jerusalem artichokes have a distinctive, comforting flavour. Caramelizing them brings out their sweet flavour which is complemented by the clean taste of soured cream. The sorrel lends a wonderful flavour to an accompanying salad and is very easy to grow. Pick off leaves from the plant as and when you need them. I have a plant in a corner of the garden and it comes up every year, even after a very cold winter, so the leaves are always to hand from spring onwards.

450g (1lb) Jerusalem artichokes, peeled
  and roughly chopped
1 red onion, peeled and finely chopped
25g (1oz) butter
1 desp olive oil
1 tbsp caster sugar

Salt and freshly ground black pepper
4 handfuls mixed leaves, such as rocket,
  lamb's lettuce and curly endive
Sprigs of parsley, finely chopped
Sprigs of sorrel, roughly torn – optional
150ml (¼ pint) soured cream

Boil the artichokes in salted water for 5 minutes then drain. Put the onion, butter, oil and caster sugar in a large frying pan and, when the butter has melted, stir in the artichokes. Cook for about 10 – 15 minutes, stirring frequently, or until the artichokes have caramelized and turned slightly brown.

Season with salt and freshly ground black pepper.

Put a handful of salad leaves on each plate with some parsley and sorrel. Spoon over the artichoke mixture and the cooking juices and top with a dollop of soured cream.

Potted Shrimps

SERVES 4

This dish has gone right out of fashion, but for no good reason. In my childhood we used to go shrimping on the Helford River in Cornwall when the tide was down and then come home to make this dish. Served with warm buttered toast and wedges of fresh lemon, it brought a satisfying end to the day.

120g (4oz) salted butter
450g (1lb) peeled cooked shrimps
Freshly grated nutmeg
Freshly ground black pepper

Pinch of cayenne pepper
120g (4oz) unsalted butter
1 tsp finely chopped parsley

Melt the salted butter in a medium-sized saucepan and add the shrimps, nutmeg, black pepper and cayenne. Warm through, stirring frequently.   Divide the mixture between four ramekins and press down well. Melt the unsalted butter in the same saucepan, add the parsley and then pour the butter over the ramekins to make the shrimps airtight. Leave to chill in the fridge until the butter sets.

Pizza-Topped Mushrooms

SERVES 4

Great big field mushrooms are a law unto themselves. They are almost like meat and have so much more flavour than their button mushroom cousins. Instead of using a pizza dough base in this recipe, the mushroom acts as the stage.

2 tbsp olive oil
1 onion, peeled and finely chopped
1 clove garlic, peeled and crushed –
  optional
1 tsp tomato purée
½ tsp chopped fresh or dried oregano
4 large flat field mushrooms, approx 15cm
  (6 inches) in diameter, wiped and stalks
  removed

12 thin slices salami
3 tomatoes, thinly sliced
1 x 125g bag Mozzarella, drained and
  sliced
Salt and freshly ground black pepper
2 tbsp grated Cheddar cheese

Preheat the oven to 200°C (400°F, Gas 6). Put the olive oil, onion and garlic into a frying pan and cook slowly for 5 minutes or until the onion is soft but not browning. Add the tomato purée and oregano, mix well, then spoon over the underside of the mushroom. Top with the slices of salami, tomato and Mozzarella, season with salt and pepper then sprinkle with the Cheddar. Place the mushrooms on an oiled baking tray and cook in the oven for about 15 minutes or until the Cheddar has melted and the mushrooms are cooked and juicy.

Egg Dishes

Eggs Benedict

SERVES 4

Without a doubt, this is my favourite egg dish. Particularly when I am working in the States and time is short, it is a great dish to order. With a bowl of French fries to dip into the extra hollandaise, it turns into perfection. If you want to make the hollandaise a little in advance, just keep it warm in a Thermos flask.

225g (8oz) butter
Juice of 1 lemon
2 egg yolks
Freshly ground black pepper

4 large eggs
2 muffins, split in half lengthways
Butter for spreading
4 slices ham

To make the hollandaise, melt the butter in a small heavy-based saucepan. Put the lemon juice, egg yolks and pepper into a liquidizer. When the butter is bubbling hot, turn on liquidizer to high and slowly pour in the butter in a constant stream. Keep blending for 30 seconds and then either pour the sauce into a warmed Thermos or leave in the liquidizer for a few minutes. Poach the large eggs either in a poacher or in salted simmering water. Toast the muffins and spread with the extra butter. Place the ham on the muffins, then place a drained poached egg on top and finally pour on the hollandaise. Serve immediately.

Omelettes

I am always amazed at the price of omelettes in restaurants — after all, they comprise of only two eggs and a filling. This is a good reason to cook them at home and they could not be easier, as long as you have a good non-stick pan.

Cheese and Tomato Omelette

SERVES 1

2 eggs
1 tsp Parmesan cheese, finely grated
1 tbsp water
Salt and freshly ground black pepper
Pinch mustard

25g (1oz) butter
Good handful grated Cheddar cheese
1 tomato, sliced
Few chives, chopped – optional

Break the eggs into a bowl. Using a fork, whisk in the Parmesan, water, salt, pepper and mustard. Melt the butter in a frying pan over a high heat and then pour in the egg mixture. Bring the edges into the middle with a fork and then reduce the heat. Sprinkle on the grated cheese then top with the tomato slices and chives. Cook for about 1 minute or until the cheese is nearly melted and the egg is still slightly runny. Tilt the pan and, folding once, tip the omelette on to a warmed plate and serve immediately.

Wild Mushroom Omelette

SERVES 2 – 4

Wild mushrooms have a special flavour, beautifully enhanced by the caramelized onions and egg mixture. This is a truly special dish.

15g (½oz) dried shitake mushrooms, or similar
1 red onion, peeled and finely chopped
1 desp sugar
1 tbsp extra virgin olive oil

1 clove garlic, peeled and crushed
1 desp wine vinegar
6 eggs
Salt and freshly ground black pepper
Small handful chives, finely chopped

Soak the mushrooms as directed on the packet, then chop roughly or cut with scissors. Put the onions and sugar into a 25cm (10 in) non-stick frying pan with the olive oil and cook slowly for 10 minutes or until slightly caramelized. Add the mushrooms, garlic and vinegar and cook for another few minutes. Remove half the mixture and set aside.

Beat the eggs in a bowl with 1 tbsp water and season with salt and pepper, then stir in the mushroom mixture from the frying pan, leaving the oil in the pan. Raise the temperature under the frying pan to a moderate heat then pour in the egg mixture. Using a fork, gently draw the uncooked egg mixture towards the centre of the pan. Cook until eggs are still slightly runny in the middle. Spread the rest of the mushroom mixture over the top. Using scissors, snip on the chives. Divide the omelette into halves or quarters, depending on your appetite, and serve.

Flipover Omelette

SERVES **4**

Spanish omelettes are very good but the potato makes them quite heavy so this version is made with other vegetables. It is very good for lunch, especially when friends drop by unexpectedly. Just raid the vegetable drawer and add whatever is to hand. This omelette is good served with a tomato, chive and Ricotta salad.

175g (6oz) courgettes, grated
2 spring onions, peeled and finely chopped
4 eggs
25g (1oz) Parmesan cheese, grated
Few black olives, finely chopped – optional

Salt and freshly ground black pepper
2 sprigs basil, torn up into small pieces
1 tbsp water
1 tbsp olive oil

Put all the ingredients, except the olive oil, into a bowl and whisk well. Heat the olive oil in a large non-stick frying pan then pour in the egg mixture. Bring the outside edge of the mixture into the middle with a fork then leave over a low heat for a few minutes or until turning golden brown on the underside. Turn over, by flipping the omelette on to a baking tray and sliding it back into the pan. Cook for another few minutes to brown again. Serve warm.

Fried Bread, Scrambled Egg and Bacon

SERVES **4**

Crispy bread with creamy eggs and crunchy bacon is one of the great British dishes and long may it last! It can be served at any time of the day but is best at breakfast in my view. Another very good accompaniment to scrambled eggs is smoked salmon. Use 50g (2oz) smoked salmon per person, top with warm scrambled egg then grind over plenty of black pepper. It makes an excellent supper dish or smart dinner-party starter.

8 rashers back bacon, rind removed if
  wished
Oil for frying
4 slices brown or white bread

4 eggs
2 tbsp milk
25g (1oz) butter
Salt and freshly ground black pepper

Put the rashers of bacon and a little oil into a large frying pan and cook gently for about 5 minutes or until the bacon is crispy. Remove and keep warm. Add the slices of bread and a little extra oil if needed and fry until the bread is golden brown on both sides. Remove and keep warm.

To make the scrambled eggs, put the eggs, milk, butter and pepper into a small heavy - based saucepan. Place over a medium heat and cook, stirring continuously, until the eggs are runny but creamy. Remember to stop cooking the eggs early as they go on cooking in the saucepan. Add a little salt to taste, remembering the bacon is salty.

Put the fried bread on warmed plates, top with the scrambled eggs and then two rashers of bacon per person. Serve hot.

Smoked Cod and Sweetcorn Soufflé

SERVES 4 - 6

Savoury soufflés are easy to cook and, as long as everyone is ready to eat them the moment they come out of the oven, they are almost fool-proof! Serve any of the following soufflés with a good French leaf salad, a Spanish tomato salad with fresh chives and perhaps some garlic bread.

175g (6oz) smoked cod,
300ml (½ pint) milk, plus a little extra
35g (1½oz) butter
35g (1½oz) flour
25g (1oz) Cheddar cheese, grated

½ a 425g (15oz) tin creamed sweetcorn
¼ tsp mustard
Freshly ground black pepper
6 eggs, separated

Preheat the oven to 200°C (400°F, Gas 6). Put the cod and milk into a saucepan and simmer for 5 minutes or until the fish is cooked. Strain off the milk into a measuring jug and make it up to 300ml (1/2 pint) with extra milk if necessary.

When the fish is cool, remove the skin and any bones then flake the flesh into a bowl. Heat the butter in a saucepan, add the flour and stir to make a roux. Pour in the fishy milk, stirring continuously to make a smooth white sauce. Remove from the heat and add the grated cheese, creamed sweetcorn, mustard, cooked fish, pepper and egg yolks (no salt should be added as the fish is salty).

Whisk the egg whites until stiff then, using a large metal spoon, fold in the fish mixture. Pour into a large buttered soufflé dish and cook for 25 minutes or until well risen, golden brown on top and still slightly wobbly. For absolute perfection, the soufflé should be slightly runny inside.

Cheese and Bacon Soufflé

SERVES 4

Bacon, eggs and cheese marry very well and the mustard used in this recipe seems to give the cheese a better, stronger flavour.

6 rashers back bacon, rind removed
35g (1½oz) butter
35g (1½oz) flour
300ml (½ pint) milk

50g (2oz) Gruyère cheese, grated
½ tsp mustard
Salt and freshly ground black pepper
4 large eggs, separated

Preheat the oven to 190°C (375°F, Gas 5). Grill or fry the rashers of bacon until very crisp. Leave to cool and then chop finely. Melt the butter in a saucepan, add the flour and stir to make a roux. Pour in the milk, stirring continuously to make a smooth white sauce. Add the cheese and stir again until melted. Remove from the heat and add the mustard, bacon pieces, salt, pepper and the egg yolks. Stir well.

Whisk the egg whites until stiff and then, using a large metal spoon, fold in the sauce mixture. Pour into a large buttered soufflé dish and cook for about 20 minutes or until well risen, golden brown and still slightly wobbly. For absolute perfection, the soufflé should still be slightly runny inside.

Mediterranean Soufflé

SERVES **4**

I made this up one evening when a vegetarian friend was coming to stay but arriving very late. It was a good light dish and the flavours worked remarkably well. The black olive paste gives the basic flavour and the chunks of Feta cheese are surprisingly fresh-tasting.

35g (1½oz) butter
35g (1½oz) flour
300ml (½ pint) milk
50g (2oz) Feta cheese, finely crumbled
1 tbsp sun-dried tomatoes in oil, finely
 chopped

6 anchovies packed in oil, finely chopped
1 desp black olive paste
4 large eggs
Freshly ground black pepper

Preheat the oven to 190°C (375°F, Gas 5). Melt the butter in a saucepan, add the flour and stir to make a roux. Pour in the milk stirring continuously to make a smooth white sauce. Remove from the heat and stir in the Feta cheese, sun-dried tomatoes, anchovies, olive paste, egg yolks and pepper. Whisk the egg whites until stiff and then, using a large metal spoon, fold the whites into the sauce mixture. Pour into a large buttered soufflé dish and cook for 20 minutes or until well risen, golden brown on top and still slightly wobbly. For absolute perfection, the soufflé should still be slightly runny inside.

Main Course Dishes

Scallops in Ginger Wine

SERVES 4

Coquilles St Jacques is a very old recipe but too creamy for my taste so I have taken the idea and exchanged the creamy sauce for a clear ginger stock. This makes a great starter or supper dish. Use scallop shells if possible, but if not, ramekin dishes will do. Adding celeriac to the potato really complements the flavour of the scallops. Add a little cream to the hot mash mixture to make it easier to pipe.

4 spring onions, peeled and finely chopped
1 desp olive oil
8 large or 12 medium scallops
1 tbsp ginger wine

Salt and freshly ground black pepper
225g (8oz) creamy mashed potato and
   celeriac mix – see page 68

Put the spring onions and oil into a frying pan and sweat for 3 minutes. Add the scallops and ginger wine and cook for about 2 minutes over a low heat or until just cooked. Season with salt and pepper. Place the scallops in the shells or ramekins. Reduce the sauce by boiling it for a few minutes if necessary. Put the hot potato and celeriac mash into a piping bag and pipe it round the edge of the shell or dish. Pour in the reduced sauce and serve.

Corned Beef Hash

SERVES **4**

I had forgotten all about this dish until my flat-mate came back one evening from the supermarket with an armful of corned beef tins. It was our staple diet for the next week or so. A truly consoling dish — delicious served with a poached egg on top.

700g (1½ lbs) potatoes, peeled and diced
Salt 50g (2oz) butter
Milk for mashing
Freshly ground black pepper
350g (12oz) tin corned beef

2 medium onions, peeled and sliced
Oil for frying
Good homemade or bought chutney —
   optional

Preheat the oven to 200C (400F, Gas 6). Boil the potatoes in salted water for 20 minutes or until soft. Drain and return to the saucepan. Add the butter and as much milk as you need to make the mash fluffy and smooth. Season to taste with pepper then, using a fork, roughly mash in the corned beef. Put the mixture into an ovenproof dish and bake for 10 minutes. Meanwhile, fry the onions in the oil until soft and serve with the hot hash and some chutney.

Cauliflower Cheese

SERVES 4

The cheese in this dish can be varied to change the flavour — try Gorgonzola or Shropshire Blue. I have stuck to the basic version here, but fried mushrooms, strips of ham, roasted peppers and so on can be added. Elaborate as you wish.

1 large fresh cauliflower, leaves removed
40g (1½oz) butter
40g (1½oz) flour
300ml (½ pint) milk
120g (4oz) strong Cheddar cheese, grated

Salt and freshly ground black pepper
½ tsp mustard
Pinch cayenne pepper
Freshly grated nutmeg

Preheat the grill to the highest setting. Cut the cauliflower into four and boil it in salted water for about eight minutes or until just beginning to soften. Drain. Melt the butter in a small saucepan and then add the flour, stirring to make a roux. Add the milk and stir to make a smooth white sauce. Add the remaining ingredients and stir over a low heat until the cheese is melted. Put the cauliflower into an ovenproof dish and pour on the cheese sauce. Place under the hot grill for a few minutes or until golden brown. Serve hot.

Freezer friendly

Mixed Cheese Fondue

SERVES 4

This is great for a cosy evening with friends and not too much effort. The Swiss say that whoever loses their bread in the cheese mixture has to kiss the person beside them, so work out who you are going to sit beside and then play your cards right. For total luxury dip your bread in kirsch and then into the cheese mixture. St André is a triple-crème cheese with a white downy rind. If you cannot find it, use another triple-crème cheese or a soft Brie instead.

1 clove garlic, halved
175g (6oz) Cheddar cheese, grated
175g (6oz) Gruyère cheese, grated
175g (6oz) St André cheese, diced
300ml (½ pint) dry white wine
2 tsp cornflour

2 tbsp kirsch
Freshly ground black pepper
Freshly grated nutmeg
1 small loaf soft white bread, cut into bite-sized pieces

Rub a heavy saucepan or a fondue pot with the garlic. Put the cheeses and the wine into the pan or pot and stir. Put over a low heat and stir until the cheeses are completely melted. Mix the cornflour and kirsch in a cup and then add to the cheese mixture, season with pepper and nutmeg and continue to cook over a very low heat, stirring continuously until thick and smooth. At the table, keep the fondue warm and stir it periodically. Each diner takes turns to spear the bread cubes on the end of a fork and dip them into the cheese mixture before eating.

Stuffed Marrow

SERVES **6**

This is a cheap and gratifying dish but sadly often forgotten. It is also a good way to use those homegrown courgettes that ran wild while you were on holiday.

1 whole tender marrow, about 900g (2 lbs)
1 onion, peeled and finely chopped
1 clove garlic, peeled and crushed
450g (1lb) minced meat – lamb or beef
25g (1oz) flour
1 tsp tomato purée
½ tsp fresh or dried oregano
Salt and freshly ground black pepper
Few drops Tabasco
1 tsp Worcestershire sauce

Splash red wine – optional

For the sauce:
25g (1oz) butter
25g (1oz) flour
150ml (½pint) milk
50g (2oz) Cheshire cheese, grated
Mustard to taste
Handful fresh parsley, finely chopped
Salt and freshly ground black pepper

Preheat the oven to 190°C (375°F, Gas 5). Cut the marrow in half and remove the seeds. Place on a baking tray. Fry the onion and garlic slowly for 5 minutes or until soft but not browning, then add the meat and stir well. Add the flour and the remaining ingredients, along with a little water if you are not using red wine. Cook slowly for about 5 minutes to infuse the flavours. Spoon the mixture into the middle of the marrow halves and smooth over.

To make the sauce, melt the butter in a small saucepan, add the flour and stir to make a roux. Add the milk and stir to make a smooth white sauce. Add the cheese and season with the mustard, salt and pepper. Cook over a low heat until the cheese has melted and then spoon the sauce over the top of the marrow. Bake in the oven for 35 minutes or until the marrow is soft and the cheese sauce is lightly browned. Sprinkle with the parsley and serve hot.

Multi-Storey Pizza

SERVES 6

When you smell this pizza cooking you will feel that you are in the hills near Naples — just open a bottle of Italian red wine and the scene will be perfection. This recipe is far superior to the combination of bought pizza base and DIY topping. The filling oozes its flavour through the dough and the sides rise to the occasion to become crispy and light. It is a must to try that will not disappoint.

For the dough:
7g (¼ oz) packet active dried yeast
450g (1lb) white flour
1 tsp salt
Olive oil for frying
1 desp oregano leaves, fresh or dried
1 tbsp freshly grated Parmesan cheese
2 tbsp cornmeal

For the topping:
1 red onion, peeled and sliced
1 clove garlic, peeled and crushed
1 small aubergine, thinly sliced
Salt and freshly ground black pepper
1 tbsp virgin olive oil
1 tbsp tomato purée
900g (2lbs) plum tomatoes, skinned and
  sliced
Handful basil leaves, torn
2 x 125g Mozzarella cheese, drained and
  sliced
Few black olives, sliced – optional

To make the dough, dissolve the yeast in 6 tablespoons of lukewarm water in a small bowl, and leave for 10 minutes. Put the flour and salt into a large bowl then pour in the yeast mixture and 200ml (⅓ pint) warm water. Stir well, first with a wooden spoon and then with your hands. Knead to a soft dough, put it in an oiled bowl and leave covered in a warm place for about three hours.

Preheat the oven to 230°C (450°F, Gas 8). Sprinkle the oregano leaves, cornmeal and Parmesan onto a work surface and knead the risen dough in this mixture back to its original size. Place the dough on a generously oiled baking tray and, using your hands, stretch it into a thin 30cm (12 in) circle, slightly risen at the sides.

To make the topping, sprinkle the aubergine slices with salt and leave for a few minutes. Rinse and dry with kitchen paper. Fry the onion and garlic in about 4 tbsp of olive oil for 5 minutes then add the aubergine and continue frying over a low heat until the aubergine is beginning to soften, adding more oil if necessary. Brush the dough base with olive oil and then spread over the tomato purée. Spoon on the onion mixture, top with the slices of tomato and then sprinkle with the basil leaves. Arrange the slices of Mozzarella on top and garnish with the black olives.

Cook the pizza in the oven for about 15 minutes or until golden brown and crispy. If the edges start to brown too fast, reduce the oven temperature a little. Serve immediately.

Chicken Satay with Sauce

This is a great dish to eat in front of the telly, or you can make it on smaller sticks and serve them with drinks. Lamb, beef or pork can be substituted for the chicken. Remember that the meat is best marinated overnight, so plan ahead.

For the marinade:
3 tbsp water
1 tbsp grated root ginger
1 tsp ground coriander
1 desp Pernod – optional
½ tsp cumin
1 tsp turmeric
1 desp runny honey
2 tsp sugar
¼ tsp salt

½ stalk lemongrass
450g (1 lb) chicken meat, skinned and cut
    into 2.5cm (1 in) cubes.

For the satay sauce:
2 tsp Thai hot green curry paste
425ml (¾ pint) coconut milk
2 tbsp smooth peanut butter

To make the marinade, put all the ingredients except the lemon grass and chicken in a liquidizer and whizz until smooth. Stir in the lemongrass and chicken until well coated then cover and chill overnight.

To make the satay sauce, put the curry paste and coconut milk into a large frying pan or wok and stir well. Add the peanut butter and simmer over a low heat for 10 minutes, stirring continuously. Pour into a dish and keep warm.

To cook the meat, preheat the grill to a moderate heat and spear the meat onto kebab sticks. Grill for about 5 minutes, turning frequently, until meat is browned and cooked. Serve with the satay sauce.

Pesto Gnocchi with Sun-Dried Tomatoes

SERVES 4

Gnocchi is my all time favourite pasta and my best memory is sitting on a hot May day in the main square of Siena eating a plate of pesto gnocchi, accompanied by a bottle of Frascati and listening to the Italian language floating through the air. Imagination is a great thing when I sit in my garden in Primrose Hill!

For the gnocchi:
175g (6oz) plain flour
1 egg, beaten
Salt and freshly ground black pepper
450g (1lb) potato, peeled, cooked and
　mashed
1 heaped tbsp pesto sauce

For the sauce:
⅓ of a 285g (10oz) jar sun-dried tomatoes
　in oil
2 tbsp virgin olive oil
Small handful fresh sage, finely chopped

Put the flour, egg, salt and pepper, potato and pesto into a bowl and mix well to make a dough. Place on a floured surface and shape pieces of dough into long rolls, about 2.5cm (1in) thick. Cut into 3.5cm (1½in) lengths and curve each of them by pressing with your finger.

Bring a large pan of boiling salted water to simmering point and cook the gnocchi in small batches for 3 – 4 minutes. They will conveniently rise to the surface when cooked. Remove with a slotted spoon, drain and keep warm.

To make the sauce, chop up the sun-dried tomatoes and put them in a saucepan with 1 tablespoon of oil from the jar, the virgin olive oil and the chopped sage. Warm through and pour over the gnocchi. Serve with a good herby French leaf salad.

Freezer friendly

Skate Wings with Lemon Butter

SERVES 2

Skate is an incredibly underrated fish and I can't think why. The flesh has an excellent flavour, the bones are easy to eat from and it is not expensive to buy. This is an excellent dish when you have been feeling poorly, but if that is the case, cut down on the sauce.

450g (1 lb) skate wing, cut in half
1 large knob butter
Juice of 1 lemon

Small handful parsley, chopped
Salt and freshly ground black pepper

Put the skate in a large saucepan of warm salted water and bring to the boil. Reduce the heat and simmer for 10 minutes. Drain the fish and keep warm.

In a small saucepan, melt the butter, add the lemon juice and parsley and season with salt and pepper. Put the skate on serving plates and pour on the butter sauce. Serve with mashed potato and cooked broccoli.

Roti with Spicy Beef

SERVES **4**

When I arrive on Bequia, my favourite island in the Caribbean, the second thing I do is go to a local café and eat a goat roti. This is the English equivalent, and apart from the weather, I can believe I am back on the beach, with sand sifting through my toes, while eating it. Jalapeno sauce has a sweeter, milder flavour than Tabasco and is well worth adding. It can be found in most major supermarkets.

I tbsp olive oil
I onion, peeled and finely chopped
I clove garlic, peeled and crushed
450g (1lb) rump beefsteak, cut into fine
   strips
I desp flour
Salt and freshly ground black pepper
2 tomatoes, finely chopped
I desp runny honey

2 tsp jalapeno sauce
I desp soya sauce
Few drops Tabasco
I avocado, halved, stone removed, sliced
   and scooped out with a spoon
Juice of I lime
4 large flour tortillas, warmed in very low
   oven
150ml (¼ pint) soured cream

Put the oil, onion and garlic in a frying pan and cook slowly for 5 minutes or until the onion is soft but not browning. Toss the meat in seasoned flour and then add to the onions and stir-fry for about 3 minutes. Add the tomatoes, honey, jalapeno sauce, soya sauce and Tabasco and stir well. Cook for another few minutes to infuse the flavours, add the avocado and lime juice and season to taste. Spoon the mixture into the warmed tortillas, add a dollop of soured cream and roll them up like a pancake. Eat with your hands.

Roast Chicken with Black Pudding Stuffing and Bread Sauce

SERVES 5

This is the ultimate comfort roast, especially when the chicken and all the trimmings are engulfed in bread sauce.

I small black pudding, approximately 225g (6 oz)
I small cooking apple, peeled, cored and roughly chopped
1.8kg (4 lb) free-range chicken
5 rashers back bacon
Freshly ground black pepper
5 chipolata sausages – optional
I tbsp flour
300ml (½ pint) chicken stock or water

For the bread sauce:
½ onion, peeled, halved and studded with 5 cloves
300ml (½ pint) full-fat milk
2 bay leaves
50g (2oz) fresh white breadcrumbs
25g (I oz) butter
Salt and freshly ground black pepper

Preheat the oven to 200°C (400°F, Gas 6). Mix the black pudding with the apple and then use it to stuff the cavity of the chicken loosely. Place the chicken in a roasting tin and cover with the bacon rashers. Grind on some black pepper and roast in the oven for ½ hour. Add the chipolatas, if using, then continue cooking for another hour.

Meanwhile, make the bread sauce. Put the onion halves in a small saucepan with the milk and bay leaves and slowly heat to simmering point. Turn off the heat and leave to infuse for 30 minutes. Strain the milk into a jug and discard the flavourings. Return the milk to the pan and add the breadcrumbs and butter. Season with salt and pepper, then stir over a low heat, adding some more milk if mixture is too thick. Keep warm until ready to serve.

Remove the chicken from the oven and check whether it is cooked by gently pulling one of the legs away from the body – it should come away easily and no blood should run. Place the chicken on a serving dish and keep warm.

To make the gravy, drain off most of the fat from the roasting tin, reserving the meat juices, and sprinkle in the flour to soak up the remaining fat. Add the chicken stock or water and bring to the boil, stirring well. Season with salt and pepper and pour into a gravy boat. For extra indulgence, a little red or white wine can be added to the gravy if it is to hand. Serve with the chicken and bread sauce.

Shepherd's Pie

SERVES 4

There are many versions of Shepherd's Pie and, surprisingly, many contain beef and not lamb, without being heralded as Cottage Pie. 'School Shepherd's Pie' always contained diced carrots and frozen peas. I hope you will be relieved that I have omitted these colourful but naff ingredients.

1 medium onion, peeled and finely chopped
1 tbsp oil
350g (12oz) lean minced lamb or beef
2 tbsp medium oatmeal
1 tbsp flour
50ml (2fl oz) red wine – optional
Splash of meat stock or water
2 tomatoes
1 desp tomato ketchup
1 tsp Worcestershire sauce
1 tbsp fruit chutney

Salt and freshly ground black pepper
1 tsp oregano, finely chopped
1 tsp rosemary, finely chopped
350g (12oz) potatoes, peeled and roughly chopped
125g (4oz) celeriac, peeled and roughly chopped – optional
50g (2oz) butter
75ml (3fl oz) milk
50g (2oz) Cheddar cheese, grated

Preheat the oven to 200°C (400°F, Gas 6). Put the onions and oil into a saucepan and cook slowly for 5 minutes or until softened but not brown. Add the meat and stir over the heat for 1 minute. Add the oatmeal and flour, then the red wine and a little stock or water. Stir and leave to simmer very gently for about 10 minutes.

Score the tomatoes and plunge them into a bowl of boiling water for 1 minute or until the skin splits, then plunge them into cold water. Peel and chop the tomatoes finely then add them to the meat mixture with the tomato Ketchup, Worcestershire Sauce, chutney, salt, pepper and herbs and stir well. Remove from heat.

Cook the potatoes and celeriac in boiling salted water for about 20 minutes or until soft. Drain and return them to the saucepan. Add the butter, salt and pepper and mash, adding the milk a little at a time until light and fluffy. Put the meat mixture into an ovenproof dish and smooth over. Cover with the mashed potato, smoothing the top with a fork. Sprinkle on the cheese and cook in the oven for 30 minutes or until the potato is golden brown.

Freezer friendly

Steak and Kidney Pudding

SERVES **4**

This reminds me of going for a long winter's walk and coming back home to a steaming dish served with red cabbage and mashed potato. The suet crust is spongy and soaks up the gravy so well. If you wish, you could add half a 100g (3 1/2oz) tin of smoked oysters to the uncooked meat mixture to give a lovely smoky flavour. The rest of the oysters can be eaten with drinks beforehand.

For the pastry:
225g (8oz) self-raising flour
Salt
Small handful parsley, chopped
120g (4oz) shredded beef suet
Water to mix
Butter for greasing

For the filling:
675g (1½lb) rump or chuck steak, diced
225g (8oz) ox kidney, diced
1 tbsp flour
Salt and freshly ground black pepper
1 small onion, peeled and finely chopped
150ml (¼ pint) water, stock or brown ale

To make the pastry, mix the flour, salt, parsley and suet in a bowl. Add just enough water to mix to a soft dough, first with a round-bladed knife, and then with one hand. On a floured surface, roll out three-quarters of the dough into a round about 1cm (½ in) thick. Grease a 1.2 litre (2 pint) pudding basin with the butter and line it with the rolled pastry.

To make the filling, put the steak and kidney in a small plastic bag with the flour, salt and pepper, close the top and shake well to coat the meat in the flour. Add the onion and shake again. Put the meat mixture into the lined basin and then pour in the water, stock or brown ale.

Roll out the remaining pastry and cover the pudding, wetting the edges and pinching them together so the pudding is airtight. Cover the pudding with greaseproof paper and tie with string. Put it into a large saucepan and add hot water until it comes three-quarters of the way up the side of the basin. Cover tightly and simmer slowly for 3 1/2 hours, adding more water to the saucepan as needed. Serve the pudding from the basin with a posh cloth wrapped round the dish or turn out.

Roquefort and Leek Quiche

SERVES 6

Although they are generally joked about, quiches are still one of the most popular dishes and to eat one straight from the oven is a rare and delicious experience. The following recipe has a smooth texture and a good strong flavour of cheese and leeks. Serve with a tomato and chive salad.

120g (4oz) plain flour
120g (4oz) medium oatmeal
Pinch salt
120g (4oz) butter
Handful parsley, finely chopped
Water to mix
1 leek, washed and finely chopped

25g (1oz) butter, extra
175g (6oz) cream cheese
85g (3oz) Roquefort cheese, crumbled
3 eggs, beaten
300ml (½ pint) single cream
Freshly ground black pepper

Preheat the oven to 190°C (375°F, Gas 5). Put the flour, oatmeal and salt into a bowl and mix well. Add the butter in small pieces and, using your fingertips, rub until the mixture resembles breadcrumbs. Using a round-bladed knife, stir in the parsley and just enough water to make a stiff dough. Roll out the dough on a floured surface and use it to line a 20cm (8 in) flan dish. You may have to use your hands as the pastry can be very crumbly. Put the leeks into a frying pan with the extra butter and sweat until they are soft but not browned. Set aside.

In a bowl, mix the cream cheese and Roquefort until smooth. Add the beaten eggs, mix well again then add the cream, black pepper and leeks. Pour the mixture into the pastry case and cook for 30 minutes or until golden brown and set. Serve warm.

Freezer friendly

Madame Bubble and Squeak

SERVES 4

I have given this comfort food favourite the title of Madame because it is topped with a fried egg — the yolk makes a delicious sauce.

1 tbsp beef dripping or butter
1 onion, peeled and finely chopped
450g (1lb) cooked mashed potato
225g (8oz) cooked green cabbage,
   chopped

Oil for frying
4 eggs

In a large frying pan, melt the dripping or butter and add the onion. Cook for 5 minutes or until soft but not browning. Add the potato and cabbage and mix well together. Flatten the mixture in the pan and cook for 3 minutes or until browned underneath. Slide out on to a board and return to the pan upside down. Cook for a further 3 minutes or until browned and then slide on to a warmed serving dish. Add a little oil to the pan and break in each egg. Fry over a medium heat until the whites are cooked but the yolks are runny. Lift out and place carefully on the Bubble and Squeak without breaking the yolks. Cut into four, avoiding the eggs, and serve. If no one is looking, eat with tomato ketchup!

Roast Rib of Beef with Yorkshire Pudding

SERVES **8**

Beef cooked on the bone has the luxury of extra flavour and although harder to carve, is well worth the extra effort. The larger the joint, the more crispy bits and wonderful juices it has so ask some friends round. Yorkshire pudding is essential with this dish and I find that making it in little cups means virtually no risk of failure.

Approximately 1.8kg (4lbs) rib roast beef
   on the bone
1 tbsp flour
300ml (½ pint) water or vegetable water
Salt and freshly ground black pepper

For the Yorkshire puddings:
120g (4oz) self-raising flour
Pinch salt
2 eggs
300ml (½ pint) mixture of half milk, half
   water

Preheat the oven to 220°C (425°F, Gas 7). Weigh the beef and put it in a large roasting tin to cook for 30 minutes, then turn the oven down to 190°C (375°F, Gas 5) and cook for a further fifteen minutes per 450g (1lb) for rare and 20 minutes per 450g (1lb) for medium-well done.

Meanwhile, to make the Yorkshire pudding, put the flour, salt, eggs and milk into a liquidizer and blend for 30 seconds on high. Leave to stand for 30 minutes then transfer into a good pouring jug. Half an hour before the meat is cooked, drain some of the beef fat from the roasting tin and pour a little into each of the 8 baking cups. Pour in the Yorkshire pudding batter and place the cups on the top shelf of the oven for 15 – 20 minutes or until golden brown and well risen.

To make the gravy, put the roast on a serving dish and drain off most of the fat, leaving the brown meat juices. Stir in the flour and then add the water or vegetable water. Bring to the boil, stirring continuously until smooth. Season with salt and pepper and pour into a gravy boat. Serve the gravy alongside the beef and Yorkshire puddings.

Pot au Feu

SERVES **8**

The late Theo Cowan, well-known PR man to the rich and famous, regularly had a 'boil up' on Sunday evenings. He said it was very therapeutic, adding to the pot all afternoon while gardening in summer or organising his desk in winter, ending up with a comforting reward at the end of the day.

900g (2lb) shin of beef, bones cut up
900g (2lb) topside, tied tightly to keep
  shape
225g (8oz) calves' liver
3 litres (5¼ pints) meat stock or water
3 carrots, peeled and cut into chunks
1 turnip, peeled and cut into chunks

2 leeks, washed well and sliced
4 sticks celery, washed and roughly
  chopped
Salt and freshly ground black pepper
1 bouquet garni
1 large cabbage, tough outer leaves
  removed then cut into eight

Put the shin bones in a large heavy-based saucepan and then add the meats. Cover with the meat stock or water and bring very slowly to simmering point (this will prevent the meat becoming tough). When the liquid is about to simmer, turn the heat down to the lowest setting. Using a slotted spoon, remove any scum from the surface. Repeat this when necessary. Simmer very slowly for 1½ hours, then add all the vegetables except the cabbage. Season with salt, pepper and add the bouquet garni. Continue simmering very slowly for another hour. Add the cabbage and simmer for a final hour. Serve the meat, vegetables and broth in deep dishes, accompanied by French bread.

Fish Cakes with Dill Sauce

SERVES 6

A variety of fish such as can be used. I have chosen huss because it is cheap and underrated, and the smoked cod because it has fewer bones than haddock. For a change, try fennel instead of celeriac or, for the plain eaters, just use potato. The sauce is lovely and light but if you prefer a richer indulgence then make the hollandaise on page 43

225g (8oz) huss or cod
225g (8oz) smoked cod
225g (8oz) potatoes, peeled and chopped
120g (4oz) celeriac, peeled and finely
   chopped
25g (1oz) butter
2 eggs, separated
1 spring onion, finely chopped – optional

Handful parsley, finely chopped
Freshly ground black pepper
Juice of ½ lemon
150ml (¼ pint) crème fraîche
Small handful dill, chopped finely
Flour for dusting
120g (4oz) fresh white breadcrumbs
Oil for frying

Put the fish into a saucepan, add some water, then cover and poach over a low heat for about 10 minutes or until the fish is cooked. Leave to cool then skin and debone the fish. Discard the liquid. Meanwhile, cook the potatoes and celeriac in salted water for about 20 minutes or until soft, then drain. Mash well.

Melt the butter in a large pan and stir in the fish, potatoes, egg yolks, spring onion and parsley until well blended. Season with pepper and stir in the lemon juice. Leave to cool.

Make the sauce by mixing the crème fraîche with the chopped dill and put it into a serving dish. Divide the fish and potato mixture into 12 and then, using floured hands, shape into small patties. Dip the cakes in the egg whites and coat them with the breadcrumbs. Heat the oil in a frying pan and fry four cakes at a time over a medium heat, turning after 5 minutes or when the underside is golden brown. Repeat on the other side and serve hot with the chilled sauce.

Freezer friendly – fishcakes only

Kedgeree

SERVES 6

Very few recipes for kedgeree are as gratifying as this one. I think it needs all the extra ingredients, such as bacon and the cheese sauce, to transform it into something really special. Kedgeree is known as a brunch-style meal but it is great for a dinner party served with a colourful tomato and basil salad.

450g (1lb) smoked cod
600ml (1 pint) mixture of half milk, half water
1 tbsp cooking oil
1 onion, peeled and finely chopped
175g (6oz) long grain rice
6 rashers streaky bacon, grilled until crisp, then chopped

3 hard-boiled eggs, shelled and roughly chopped
Handful parsley, finely chopped
Freshly ground black pepper
25g (1oz) butter
25g (1oz) flour
85g (3oz) Cheddar cheese, grated
½ tsp mustard

Poach the fish in a covered saucepan with the milk and water mixture for about 10 minutes or until the fish is cooked. Strain and reserve the juices. When the fish is cool, remove and discard the skin and bones and reserve the flesh. Put the oil in a large saucepan, add the onion and cook slowly for about five minutes or until the onion is soft but not browning. Add the rice, stir well and then add half the milk mixture. Cook the rice over a low heat, adding more water if necessary, for about 20 minutes or until the rice is soft. The rice should be only slightly wet when fully cooked. Add the crispy

bacon pieces, hard boiled eggs, parsley, pepper and fish. Stir well and keep warm.

To make the sauce, melt the butter in a small saucepan, add the flour and stir to make a roux. Slowly add the remaining milk and water mixture, stirring continuously to make a smooth white sauce. Add the cheese and mustard and some pepper. Stir over a low heat until the cheese is melted.

Put the rice mixture on to a serving plate and pour over the cheese sauce. Sprinkle on some extra chopped parsley if you wish and serve hot.

Cod Steaks with Fennel Mash

SERVES **4**

Cod is very undervalued and has a lovely subtle flavour, especially when married with this fennel mash. If you want to be more extravagant, halibut or turbot can be used instead. The mash must be cooked at the last minute as reheating will diminish the flavour of the fennel. This dish could not be easier and is perfect served for supper or as the main course for a dinner party. Serve with a green leaf and fresh herb salad, using coriander, basil and parsley.

680g (1½ lbs) potatoes, peeled and roughly chopped
1 fennel bulb, trimmed and finely chopped
Salt and freshly ground black pepper

1½ tbsp olive oil
2 tbsp milk
4 thick cod fillets
Olive oil for frying

Cook the potatoes in boiling salted water for about 15 minutes or until soft.   Meanwhile, boil the fennel in salted water for 1 minute then drain. Drain the potatoes and mash them with the pepper, olive oil and milk until light and fluffy. Stir in the fennel.

To cook the fish, heat a little oil in a large frying pan and fry the cod fillets for 3 – 4 minutes on each side or until the fish is just cooked. Spoon the mash on to dinner plates, place a fillet on top then pour over the cooking juices.

Calves' Sweetbreads with Parsley Sauce

SERVES 4 - 6

This is one of the most old fashioned recipes in this book but also one of my favourites. Its very mild flavour makes it a good dish for anyone needing gentle comfort.

680g (1½ lbs) calves' sweetbreads
25g (1oz) butter
25g (1oz) flour

300ml (½ pint) milk
Salt and freshly ground black pepper
Handful parsley, finely chopped

Put the sweetbreads into a saucepan of warm water and slowly bring to simmering point. Simmer over a very low heat for 15 minutes. Skim the scum from the surface using a slotted spoon, then strain. Remove any membranes from the sweetbreads.

To make the white sauce, melt the butter in a saucepan and then stir in the flour to make a roux. Add the milk stirring continuously to make a smooth white sauce. Season with the salt, pepper and parsley. Add the sweetbreads to the sauce and serve hot.

Lamb's Liver with Tomato and Yoghurt

SERVES 4

This is one of the quickest dishes to make and, because of this, it is the one I cook most often. I keep some livers in the freezer, have a tube of tomato purée in the cupboard and, more often than not, have some plain yoghurt in the fridge – and that is it!

450g (1lb) lamb's livers
Flour for dusting
Salt and freshly ground black pepper
Oil for frying

1 onion, peeled and finely chopped –
    optional
Good squirt tomato purée
150ml (¼ pint) plain yoghurt

Season the flour with salt and pepper and use it to coat the lamb's livers. Heat the oil in a frying pan, add the onions, if using, and fry for 5 minutes or until soft but not brown. Reduce the heat and add the livers. Cook for about 2 minutes on one side then turn over. Add the tomato purée and yoghurt and stir well. Depending on how rare you like your meat, remove immediately or cook for another few minutes.

Baked Potatoes

Baked potatoes are my mainstay in winter. To me they are the ultimate comfort food. When I am feeling lazy and do not want to cook dinner, a baked potato filled with a small tin of baked beans and topped with some grated cheese is ideal, and quite a healthy meal.

Soufflé Baked Potato

SERVES 8

4 large baking potatoes, scrubbed
Oil
Salt and freshly ground black pepper
50g (2oz) butter

Milk for mashing
25g (1oz) Cheddar cheese, grated
Pinch of mustard powder
2 eggs, separated

Preheat the oven to 200°C (400°F, Gas 6). Rub each potato with oil and some salt, then prick them with a fork. Place on a baking tray or spear them onto long skewers and cook for 1 hour or until the skins are crisp and the potatoes are soft inside. Leave the oven on.

Cut the potatoes in half lengthways. Holding a hot potato half in a cloth in one hand, scoop out the flesh with a spoon into a bowl. Repeat with the remaining halves of potato. Set the skins aside. Add the butter and some milk to the bowl and mash until light and fluffy. Add the cheese, salt and pepper, mustard and the egg yolks and mash again.

Whisk the egg whites until stiff and then, using a large metal spoon, fold the whites into the mashed potato. Spoon the mixture back into the potato skins and place them on a baking tray. Cook for 20 minutes or until well risen and lightly browned. Serve immediately.

Baked Potatoes with Sour Cream and Chives

serves 6

---

6 medium-sized baking potatoes, scrubbed
Oil for rubbing
Salt
85g (3oz) butter

150ml (5floz) soured cream
Freshly ground black pepper
Handful of chives

Preheat the oven to 200°C (400°F, Gas 6). Using your hands, rub a little oil and salt on the potato skins then prick them with a fork. Place on a baking tray or spear onto long skewers. Bake for 1 hour or until the skins are crisp and the potatoes are soft inside. Cut a large cross in the top of each cooked potato and squeeze open. Divide the butter into six pieces and put a knob inside each potato. Top with soured cream and pepper then, using scissors, snip the chives over the top. Serve hot.

Bangers and Mash
with Fried Onions

SERVES 4

I love baked beans and always add a splash of port or red wine to boost their flavour. This recipe cries out for just such an accompaniment. There are so many good sausage flavours now available that you should choose your own, but I love pork and apple or a good Cumberland, if you need a guide.

8 large sausages
2 medium onions, thinly sliced
Oil for frying
450g (1lb) potatoes, peeled and chopped
225g (8oz) celeriac, peeled and finely
  chopped

Salt and freshly ground black pepper
25g (1oz) butter
125ml (4floz) full-fat milk
Freshly grated nutmeg

Put the sausages under a medium grill and cook for 10 – 15 minutes, turning four times during cooking to brown them completely. Put the sliced onion in a frying pan with a little oil and cook gently for 5 minutes or until soft and slightly browned. Meanwhile, boil the the potatoes and celeriac in salted water for about 20 minutes or until soft, then drain. Return to the saucepan, add the butter and milk and mash until smooth and fluffy. Sprinkle with nutmeg and serve with the sausages and onions – not forgetting the baked beans.

Fish Pie

SERVES 6 - 8

This fish pie has got the lot. You can vary it to your taste and if you prefer, top it with mashed potato. I have used frozen shellfish for convenience but if you are near the coast and have the time, fresh seafood would be better.

450g (1 lb) smoked cod
600ml (1 pint) milk
1 onion, peeled and finely chopped
5 rashers streaky bacon, rind removed and
  chopped – optional
50g (2oz) butter
50g (2oz) flour
2 hard-boiled eggs, shelled and chopped
1 red pepper, deseeded and finely chopped
Juice of 1 lemon
1 tsp mustard

Few drops Tabasco
Large handful parsley, finely chopped
120g (4oz) frozen cockles, thawed and
  drained
120g (4oz) frozen mussels, thawed and
  drained
120g (4oz) frozen shelled prawns, thawed
  and drained
375g (13oz) tin smoked oysters, drained
375g (13oz) puff pastry
Glaze: 1 egg beaten with 2 tsp milk

Preheat the oven to 200°C (400°F, Gas 6). Put the cod in a saucepan with the milk, bring slowly to the boil, cover and simmer for 5 minutes. Remove from the heat and strain, reserving the milk. Fry the onion with the bacon, if using, for 5 minutes or until soft but not brown, then remove with a slotted spoon and reserve. Melt the butter in a saucepan, stir in the flour to make a roux and then gradually add the milk from the fish, stirring continuously, to make a smooth sauce. Add the hard-boiled egg, onion and bacon, red pepper, lemon juice, mustard, all the shellfish and the cod and mix well.

Pour into a 31cm (12in) pie dish. Roll out the pastry to the size of the pie dish, wet the rim of the dish and top with the pastry. Trim the edge of the pastry with a knife, press down carefully with a fork to make a pattern and then brush the surface with the beaten egg glaze. Make little fish shapes with the leftover pastry if you wish and use them to decorate the pastry lid, glazing them with the egg wash. Cook in the oven for 30 minutes or until the pastry is golden brown and well risen. Serve hot.

Three-Tomato Risotto with Goat Cheese

SERVES **8** AS A STARTER OR **4** FOR A MAIN COURSE

This risotto has a marvellous sticky, cheesy sauce to bind each rice grain and keep it moist. Try to use homemade stock in this recipe if you can — it is worth the effort. The three types of tomato give the risotto a fresh, colourful frame. Very good as a starter or main course.

425ml (¾ pint) chicken stock
50g (2oz) butter
1 small red onion, peeled and finely
   chopped
285g (10oz) risotto rice, preferably arborio
150ml (¼ pint) white wine
50g (2oz) Parmesan cheese, freshly grated
½ a 280g (10oz) jar sun-dried tomatoes in

oil, finely chopped
Small handful fresh mint, finely chopped
Salt and freshly ground black pepper
3 red tomatoes
8 yellow tomatoes
8 slices goat cheese log, 1cm (½in) thick,
   7½cm (3in) diameter

Heat the stock in a saucepan. Melt the butter in a large heavy-based saucepan, add the onion and cook slowly for five minutes or until soft but not browning. Add the rice and stir well to coat in butter. Add the stock and wine and stir well. Bring to simmering point and cook gently for about 20 minutes or until the rice is soft and the liquid nearly all absorbed. Add the Parmesan, sun-dried

tomatoes, mint and then season to taste.

Skin the red tomatoes by pricking the skin and then plunging them into boiling water. Leave until the skin splits (about 20 seconds) and then run under cold water. The skins should now come off easily. Cut red tomatoes in half, remove the pips and then chop finely. Slice the yellow tomatoes thinly.

Preheat the grill to high. Spoon eight piles

of risotto on to a flat grill pan and place a slice of goat cheese on each. Grill for a few minutes or until the cheese is just starting to brown. Place the risotto piles on eight plates, top each goat cheese with some chopped red tomatoes, and arrange the yellow tomato slices round each plate like petals. Sprinkle with rock salt and freshly ground black pepper and serve.

Macaroni Cheese

SERVES 4

I have slightly elaborated this dish to give it more flavour. If asparagus is out of season then you could use small florets of blanched broccoli. Vegetarians can simply omit the ham. It can make a perfect supper dish served with a tomato and chive salad.

350g (12oz) macaroni,
25g (1oz) butter
25g (1oz) flour
300ml (½ pint) milk
Salt and freshly ground black pepper
½ tsp English mustard

85g (3oz) Cheddar cheese, grated
25g (1oz) Parmesan cheese, grated
50g (2oz) home-cooked ham, diced
20 asparagus tips, blanched
25g (1 oz) white breadcrumbs
Small handful parsley, finely chopped

Preheat the oven to 190°C (375°F, Gas 5). Cook the macaroni in plenty of boiling salted water as instructed on the packet, then drain. Melt the butter in a saucepan, add the flour and stir to make a roux. Gradually add the milk, stirring continuously to make smooth white sauce. Season with a little salt (bearing in mind the ham and cheese are salty) and pepper and then add the mustard, Cheddar, Parmesan, ham, asparagus and the macaroni. Stir carefully then pour into an ovenproof dish. Mix the breadcrumbs and parsley together and sprinkle over the top. Cook in the oven for 25 minutes or until golden brown.

Freezer friendly

The Quickie Pasta Dish

SERVES **4**

After a long day's work, I often arrive home ravenous but lack the necessary energy to cook. This is the answer and one of my most-used recipes. Lovely flavours, instant energy and all using ingredients from the store cupboard. When I pass my favourite Italian shop in Fleet Road, Hampstead, I buy their fresh pasta and keep it in air-tight bags in the freezer ready for these low-energy evenings.

350g (12oz) tagliatelle, fresh or dried
Salt and freshly ground black pepper
2 tbsp virgin olive oil
Small handful fresh sage

¼ of 280g (10oz) jar sun-dried tomatoes in olive oil
50g (2oz) pine nuts
25g (1 oz) Parmesan cheese, shaved

Bring a large saucepan of salted water to the boil and add the tagliatelle. Simmer for 3 minutes if fresh, or according to the packet instructions if dried. Meanwhile, put the olive oil, sage, sun-dried tomatoes and pine nuts in a liquidizer and process for 1 minute. Drain the pasta and return it to the pan. Add the blended sauce mixture, toss gently, then spoon on to serving plates and top with the shaved Parmesan.

Navarin of Lamb

SERVES 6 - 8

This lovely warming casserole has a sweetness in the cooking juices that brings out all the fresh flavours of the other ingredients. If you have fresh herbs, make your own bouquet garni by tying a sprig of rosemary, oregano and thyme together with string.

50g (2oz) butter
900g (2lb) shoulder or leg lamb, cubed
Salt and freshly ground pepper
1 tbsp sugar
1 tbsp flour
300ml (½ pint) beef stock
2 cloves garlic, peeled and crushed
1 heaped tbsp tomato purée
1 bouquet garni
2 bay leaves
450g (1lb) baby new potatoes, scrubbed

225g (8oz) baby carrots, trimmed
225g (8oz) shallots, peeled and left whole

For the herb dumplings:
50g (2oz) self-raising flour
50g (2oz) fine breadcrumbs
2 tbsp shredded suet
Handful parsley, finely chopped
1 tsp rosemary, finely chopped
Salt and freshly ground black pepper
1 egg

Preheat the oven to 180°C (350°F, Gas 4). Melt the butter in a large ovenproof casserole dish and add the meat, salt and pepper. Stir well to brown the meat on all sides, then remove and set aside. Add the sugar to the casserole and brown gently to make a caramel. Return the meat to the casserole, add the flour and stir well. Add the stock, garlic, tomato purée, bouquet garni and bay leaves and stir well again. Cover and cook for 1 hour.

Meanwhile, to make the dumplings, mix the flour, breadcrumbs, suet, chopped herbs, seasoning and egg together and, using your hands, roll into walnut-sized balls.

After 1 hour of cooking, remove the casserole from the oven and add the potatoes, carrots, shallots and dumplings then return to the oven and cook for a further 40 minutes. Check the vegetables are cooked then serve.

Freezer friendly

Fish and Chips

SERVES **4**

We have all been brought up with the naughty treat of this take away, but quite often the chips are soggy and it is only because they are nestling in newspaper that we find them acceptable. Here's your chance to make the perfect fish dinner. I have used beer in the batter to give a good nutty flavour but, if you prefer, use water. Don't forget the vinegar and ketchup!

For the batter:
225g (8oz) flour
I can brown ale
½ tsp baking powder
Salt

600ml (I pint) vegetable oil, plus a little extra
680g (1½ lbs) potatoes, peeled and cut into chips
4 fresh cod fillets, skinned

To make the batter, mix the flour, ale, baking powder and salt in a bowl and leave to stand for 20 minutes.

Preheat the oven to 150°C (300°F, Gas 2).

To cook the fish and chips, heat the oil in a deep-fryer to 190°C (375°F). Rinse the chips in cold water and dry with kitchen paper. Fry the chips a portion at a time so the oil temperature is not reduced too much. Cook until light brown then remove from the oil. Leave for a minute then return to the hot oil and fry again until golden brown. Remove the chips from the oil and drain on kitchen paper. Keep warm in the oven. Repeat until all the chips are cooked, adding more oil if necessary and reheating it to the original temperature.

To cook the fish, dry the fillets with kitchen paper then dip them in the batter, making sure they are evenly coated. Gently lower the fish into the oil and cook for 3 – 4 minutes or until the batter turns golden brown. Serve with the hot chips.

Toad in the Hole

SERVES 6

This used to be a rather ordinary dish but now that there are so many wonderful homemade-style sausages around it has been transformed. A great supper dish, for real comfort it should be served with mushy peas or baked beans.

225g (8oz) flour
Salt
2 eggs

700ml (1¼ pints) milk
1 desp oil
450g (1lb) sausages, any flavour

Preheat the oven to 220°C (425°F, Gas 7). To make the batter, put the flour, salt, eggs and milk into a liquidizer and process on high for 30 seconds. Leave to stand for 20 minutes.

Heat the oil in a frying pan and cook the sausages gently until golden brown all over.

Pour the oil from the frying pan into a baking tin and place it in the oven for 1 minute. Arrange the sausages in the hot tin and gently pour in the batter. Cook in the oven for 25 – 30 minutes or until the batter is well risen. Serve hot.

Tripe and Onions

SERVES 4

---

*The majority of you are going to expostulate at the appearance of
this recipe but there are a few of us who love tripe — so sorry to the
rest of you, but here we go. Serve with mashed potatoes.*

675g (1½ lbs) tripe, cut into 5cm (2in)
  pieces
600ml (1 pint) milk
300ml (½ pint) water
2 bay leaves

3 onions, peeled and finely sliced
Salt and freshly ground black pepper
35g (1½ oz) butter
50g (2oz) flour
Handful parsley, finely chopped

Put the tripe in a saucepan, cover with cold
water, bring to the boil and then drain,
discarding the water. Return the tripe to the
saucepan with the milk, water, bay leaves,
onions and seasoning. Bring to the boil, cover
and simmer over a very low heat for 3 hours.
Check the liquid periodically and add a little
more water if necessary. When the tripe is
tender, drain, reserving the liquid.

To make the sauce, melt the butter in a
saucepan, stir in the flour to make a roux and
then pour in the cooking liquid from the tripe,
stirring continuously. Add the tripe and
onions to the pan with the parsley and serve
hot.

Swarbrick Duck with Apple Sauce

SERVES 4

A crisp, succulent bird, well-cooked and nestling in a luxurious bed of vegetables, accompanied by a tart apple sauce to cut through the richness — this is the perfect roast. Serve with mashed potatoes.

1.6kg (3½ lbs) duckling
Few sprigs fresh rosemary
½ lemon
1 tbsp runny honey
Salt and freshly ground black pepper
225g (8oz) okra, halved
1 small celeriac, peeled and diced

1 medium aubergine, topped, quartered
  and sliced
For the apple sauce:
2 large Bramley apples, peeled, cored and
  sliced
Sugar to taste
Splash of calvados — optional

Preheat the oven to 200°C (400°F, Gas 6). Prick the duck all over with a fork. Stuff the cavity with the rosemary and lemon, put the duck on a wire rack in a roasting tin and place in the oven for 30 minutes. Remove the wire rack and drain off the fat. Spread the honey over the skin of the duck and sprinkle it with salt and pepper.

Put the duck in the middle of the roasting tin and surround it with the prepared vegetables. Cook for a further hour in the oven or until the duck is well-browned and crispy, tossing the vegetables once or twice to coat them with the duck fat.

Meanwhile, to make the sauce, put the apples and sugar in a saucepan and cook very slowly for about 10 minutes. If the apple starts to stick, add a little water. When the apple is soft, mash it with a wooden spoon and stir in the calvados, if using. When the duck is cooked, place it on a warmed serving dish with the vegetables and serve the apple sauce alongside.

Roast Partridge with Game Chips

SERVES 2

To many people who live in the country, this is a true comfort dish. Served with a slice of bread under the bird and game chips alongside, it is hard to deny. The bird is best slightly undercooked, leaving the breast slightly pink, as this produces more tender meat. An alternative to making game chips is to deep-fry some fresh spaghetti until golden brown. I tried it for fun one day and it worked very well.

2 rashers back bacon
2 young oven-ready partridges
1 medium onion, peeled and halved
2 slices white bread, crusts removed
Splash red wine or port
Salt and freshly ground black pepper

For the game chips:
Vegetable oil for frying
225g (8oz) potatoes, peeled and cut into
    matchstick-size strips
Salt

Preheat the oven to 190°C (375°F, Gas 5). Put the rashers of bacon over the breast of the birds and place half an onion in each cavity. Put the slices of bread in a roasting tin and place a bird on each slice. Pour in the wine or port then season with salt and pepper. Roast in the oven uncovered for 30 minutes, basting once or twice.

Meanwhile, to make the game chips, pour about 7.5cm (3 in) of oil into a large saucepan or deep-fryer and heat to 200°C (400°F, Gas 6). Rinse the pared potatoes in cold water to remove excess starch and dry with kitchen paper. Put them into the hot oil and move them around a little so they do not stick. Remove when they are golden brown, drain on kitchen paper and sprinkle with salt. Keep warm and serve with the birds.

Spicy Beef Casserole with Oranges

SERVES 8

A lovely warm spicy casserole that can be cooked in the oven while chores are done. Settle down to this dish with herbed brown rice and some crisp green broccoli.

2 tbsp olive oil
1 large onion, peeled and sliced
2 cloves garlic, peeled and crushed
1 desp dark brown sugar
900g (2lbs) chuck steak, cut into 2.5cm (1in) cubes
15cm (6in) square pork rind – optional
1 tbsp flour
16 shallots, peeled and left whole

Splash brandy
¼ stick cinnamon
Juice and grated rind of ½ orange
6 cloves stuck into the used orange half
25g (1oz) black olives, stoned and quartered
150ml (¼ pint) red wine
Salt and freshly ground pepper

Preheat the oven to 150°C (300°F, Gas 2). Put the oil into a large ovenproof casserole dish, add the onion and garlic and cook gently for 5 minutes or until the onion is soft. Add the sugar and cook for a further 2 minutes. Add the beef and pork skin, if using, and brown well. Stir in the flour then add the remaining ingredients. Stir well, cover and cook in the oven for 3 hours.

Remove the pork skin and clove-studded orange rind. If you would like the sauce to be thicker, remove the meat and put the juices over a high heat to reduce. Replace the meat and serve hot.

Freezer friendly

Thai Green Chicken Curry

SERVES 4

I did not think of curry as a comfort food until I went to a Thai restaurant behind St Martin's Lane in London and found myself returning for this dish as consolation on a hard day — now I am convinced. Serve it with noodles mixed with a little peanut butter if you like.

425ml (¾ pint) coconut milk
1 desp Thai green curry paste
4 chicken breasts, sliced
200ml (⅓ pint) water
2 dried lime leaves

120g (4oz) bamboo shoots, sliced
1 desp Thai fish sauce
1 tsp sugar
1 medium green chilli, deseeded and very
    finely chopped

Put half the coconut milk and the green curry paste into a saucepan and simmer for about 10 minutes, stirring occasionally, until oil separates from the coconut cream. Add the chicken meat and cook for about 5 minutes over a low heat. Add the rest of the ingredients, including the remaining coconut cream. Bring gently to the boil and then simmer for 5 minutes on a very low heat then serve with noodles or rice.

Freezer friendly

Puddings

Baked Apples with Banana

SERVES **4**

For perfection, these have to be cooked until they are sticky and gooey. I have added the lot to this recipe but you can simply leave out any ingredients that you do not like.
Serve hot with lashings of cream.

50g (2oz) sultanas
2 tbsp Grand Marnier
4 large cooking apples
Juice and grated rind of ½ orange
1 desp dark brown sugar

25g (1oz) walnuts, finely chopped
1 small banana, peeled and mashed
2 tbsp runny honey – optional
Sprinkling of cinnamon

Put the sultanas in a bowl with the Grand Marnier and soak for at least 1 hour or overnight. Preheat the oven to 180°C (350°F, Gas 4). Wipe the cooking apples, remove the cores and cut a sliver from the bottom if necessary to make them stand evenly.

Put the orange juice and rind into a bowl with the sugar, walnuts, soaked sultanas and banana and mix well, then use the mixture to stuff the apple cavities. Place the apples on a baking tray. If you have some mixture left over, pour it over the apples along with the honey, if using, making sure the skins are well coated. Sprinkle with the cinnamon and the bake in the oven for 45 minutes or until cooked. Be careful not to over-cook as the apples may collapse.

Steamed Ginger Pudding

SERVES 4 - 6

Steamed puddings seem to have been forgotten or deliberately mislaid for many years but it is definitely time they were put back on the menu. They are one of the most comforting foods and, as long as the portions are not excessive, your waistline will not expand — too much.

175g (6oz) self-raising flour
1 level tsp baking powder
Pinch salt
85g (3oz) white breadcrumbs
120g (4oz) shredded beef suet
120g (4oz) caster sugar

1 egg
Milk to mix
2 large pieces of ginger preserved in syrup, finely chopped
Golden syrup to taste

Put the flour, baking powder, salt, breadcrumbs, suet and caster sugar into a bowl and mix well. Add the egg and as much milk as necessary to make the mixture a soft dropping consistency.

Butter a 850ml (1½ pint) pudding basin and then put the chopped ginger in the bottom. Pour in about 1 desp of the ginger syrup, the golden syrup and then the pudding mixture. Cover the bowl with greaseproof paper and tie with string or use a strong elastic band.

Place in a large saucepan, add water to reach three-quarters of the way up the side of the basin and cover with a lid. Simmer for about 1 hour or until firm to the touch, checking the water level during cooking and topping up as necessary. Remove the greaseproof paper and turn out the pudding onto a plate. Be extremely careful as the syrup will be very hot. Serve with whipped cream.

To make a sticky chocolate steamed pudding, replace 25g (1oz) flour with cocoa and another 25g (1oz) flour with ground almonds. Instead of the chopped ginger and syrup, put 1 desp golden syrup mixed with 1 desp cocoa into the bottom of the pudding basin.

Freezer friendly

Junket

SERVES **4 - 6**

It is surprising to me that yoghurt is so popular yet junket is hardly ever eaten. I have kept this one plain but if you wish you can add a splash of brandy to the mixture. It is good eaten on its own or served with stewed fruits such as plums or rhubarb.

600ml (1 pint) full-fat milk
1 desp runny honey

1 tsp rennet
Freshly grated nutmeg

Heat the milk to blood temperature (test with a clean finger!). Add the honey and rennet and stir gently. Pour into a serving dish, sprinkle with grated nutmeg and leave to set for 2 – 3 hours at room temperature. If you are not eating the junket until later, keep it in the fridge.

Bread and Butter Pudding

SERVES 4 - 6

This pudding has more variations than any other that I know. The one I had at school was the most revolting thing I can ever remember, whereas Anton Mosimann's is the best pudding I have ever tasted. Here is my version.

6 hot cross buns, or 1 small white non-crusty loaf, sliced
50g (2oz) butter
1 banana, peeled and sliced – optional
4 eggs
120g (4oz) runny honey, warmed

Grated rind of 1 orange – optional
1 tbsp Grand Marnier – optional
850 ml (1½ pints) milk
150ml (¼ pint) double cream
Caster sugar to taste
Freshly grated nutmeg

Preheat the oven to 180°C (350°F, Gas 4). Spread the bread slices with most of the butter and use the remainder to grease a 1 litre (1¾ pint) baking dish. Layer the bread, with the banana if using, in the dish. Put the rest of the ingredients, except the caster sugar and nutmeg, into a jug and whisk well. Pour over the bread and leave to soak for 10 minutes. Sprinkle with a little caster sugar and nutmeg and cook for about 45 minutes or until the top is golden brown. Serve hot with whipped cream.

Rhubarb Crème Brûlée

SERVES 4

Crème Brûlée has never gone out of fashion and I am not surprised. However, it is very rich and I think it needs something to cut through the creaminess. I've added fruit, which provides a perfect contrast.

175g (6oz) rhubarb, roughly chopped
25g (1oz) sugar
Rind of ½ orange – optional
6 egg yolks

425ml (¾ pint) double cream
1 desp runny honey
Few drops vanilla essence
4 desp soft brown sugar

Preheat the oven to 180°C (350°F, Gas 4).

Cook the rhubarb with the sugar and orange rind, if using, in a very little water for about 10 minutes or until soft. Drain off any excess juice, discard the orange rind if using, then spoon the fruit into the bottom of four ramekins.

Beat the egg yolks in a large bowl. Put the cream, honey and vanilla essence into a saucepan and heat until nearly boiling, stirring continuously. When the mixture is just about to boil, pour quickly over the egg yolks beating well. Gently pour the custard into the ramekins.

Place the ramekins in an ovenproof tin, half-fill the tin with hot water and cook in the oven for 30 minutes or until set. Leave to cool and then chill.

Preheat the grill to the highest setting, top each ramekin with 2 teaspoons of brown sugar, covering all the custard, then caramelize under the grill, watching constantly. Remove the brûlées from the heat, chill again then serve.

Rhubarb and Orange Crumble with Oats

SERVES 6

This is where my Scots blood comes to light — I could never make a crumble without topping it with oats. They give a good crunchy flavour and are much better for you than breadcrumbs. This crumble needs to be served hot with cream, or try it with coconut ice cream, which can be found in most supermarkets.

680g (1½lbs) rhubarb
Juice and grated rind of 1 orange
50g (2oz) sugar
120g (4oz) porridge oats

50g (2oz) flour
85g (3oz) butter, softened
85g (3oz) soft brown sugar
1 tbsp finely chopped pecans or walnuts

Preheat the oven to 200°C (400°F, Gas 6). Put the rhubarb, the orange juice and rind and the sugar into a large ovenproof dish and mix well. Put the remaining ingredients into a bowl and mix well with your fingertips until the mixture is crumbly but thoroughly combined. Scatter it over the top of the fruit, smooth over and cook for about 45 minutes or until the crumble is golden on top and the fruit is cooked underneath.

Hot Chocolate and Banana Soufflé

SERVES 4

Whenever I feel lazy and do not want to spend time making a pudding, this is my stand-by. One evening, I suddenly remembered that the friends who were coming round had eaten it before, so I added the bananas to try and make it different. It worked very well. You could add fresh raspberries or orange segments if you like. Do not be afraid of hot soufflés. Make the recipe up to where you would whisk the egg whites. When you are about to serve the main course, warm the sauce carefully, quickly whisk the egg whites, fold them into the reheated chocolate mixture and cook. The dessert will then be ready when you are.

30g (1½oz) butter
50g (2oz) flour
300ml (½ pint) milk
50g (2oz) dark chocolate, coarsely grated
  or roughly chopped

25g (1oz) cocoa powder
25g (1oz) caster sugar
5 eggs, separated
1 large banana, peeled and sliced

Preheat the oven to 200°C (400°F, Gas 6). Melt the butter in a large saucepan and stir in the flour to make a roux. Add the milk to make a smooth white sauce, stirring continuously. Add the grated chocolate, cocoa powder and caster sugar and stir until thoroughly combined. Stir in the egg yolks and the banana.

Whisk the egg whites until very stiff and fold in the chocolate mixture. Quickly pour into a 1 litre (1¾pint) soufflé dish and cook for about 20 minutes or until well risen but still slightly runny inside. Serve immediately.

Baked Chocolate Custard

SERVES **4 - 6**

My mum could never do wrong when she cooked this custard and it was the best bribe to make me behave. It should be served plain with pouring cream. If you do not want it to be too rich, omit the cream and top up with milk.

425ml (¾ pint) milk
150ml (¼ pint) single cream
50g (2oz) dark chocolate

50g (2oz) caster sugar
3 eggs

Preheat the oven to 170°C (325°F, Gas 3). Heat the milk, cream, chocolate and sugar in a saucepan. Beat the eggs in a large bowl. Pour the milk mixture on to the eggs and stir well. Strain into a 1 litre (1¾ pint) ovenproof dish and stand in a baking tray. Half-fill the baking tray with hot water and bake in the oven for about 40 minutes or until set. Serve warm or cold.

Gooseberry Fool

SERVES **6**

Gooseberries have a short season so try to use them as soon as you see them in the shops. I always put some in the freezer so that this recipe can be made all year round.

450g (1lb) gooseberries, washed and
  trimmed
170g (6oz) caster sugar
3 eggs, separated
150ml (¼ pint) milk

1 tbsp custard powder
300ml (½ pint) double cream, whipped
120g (4oz) fresh raspberries – optional
Cocoa powder for dusting

Cook the gooseberries with the caster sugar over a very low heat for about 15 minutes or until cooked. Leave to cool and then rub through a sieve. Add the egg yolks to the fruit purée and stir well. Mix the milk and custard powder in a saucepan and stir over a low heat until thick (follow instructions on the custard tin). Stir the custard into the fruit purée and chill. Fold in the whipped cream and then whisk the egg whites and fold into the mixture. If using the raspberries, add them now, then pour the mixture into large glasses or a serving dish. Dust with a little cocoa powder to decorate.

Grape Brûlée

SERVES **4**

———————

This fresh-tasting pudding is a great favourite with my clients. Although it has cream, the crunch of the fruit and the caramel top prevent it being too rich. Only halve the grapes if you have time, if they are too big or if you are adding the alcohol. Add more booze to the cream — either more Grand Marnier or perhaps some amaretto — if you really want to indulge.

350g (12oz) seedless red or green grapes, halved
A generous splash of Grand Marnier

120g (4oz) dark brown sugar
1 desp caster sugar
300ml (½ pint) double cream, whipped

Put the grapes and Grand Marnier into a bowl, stir once or twice and leave to marinate. Preheat the grill to a moderate heat. Mould four 15cm (6in) squares of foil around the base of a ramekin to make four foil 'dishes'. Mix the brown sugar and caster sugar together, spoon them into the foil dishes and smooth over. Place them under the grill and, watching very carefully, grill until each 'cap' is caramelized. Remove from heat and leave to cool.

Put the marinated grapes into four ramekins, cover each one with the whipped cream and then top with a caramel 'cap'. Serve well chilled.

Chocolate Roulade with Lemon Syllabub Filling

The ultimate pudding. Chocolate roulade is slightly old hat now but it is always popular and, when filled with this lemon cream, no one could refuse it. Make the roulade the day before eating to allow time for the alcohol in the syllabub to seep into the chocolate. Advance preparation also makes the roulade easier to cut.

175g (6oz) dark chocolate
50ml (2floz) milk
6 eggs, separated
140g (5oz) caster sugar
1 desp cocoa powder

For the filling:
Juice and finely grated rind of 1 lemon
Finely grated rind of ½ orange
85g (3oz) caster sugar
1 tbsp brandy
1 tbsp white wine
300ml (½ pint) double cream
Icing sugar for dusting

Preheat the oven to 200°C (400°F, Gas 6) and line a 30 x 35cm (12in x 14in) baking tin with greaseproof paper.

Melt the chocolate with the milk in a small saucepan over a low heat, stirring until smooth. Whisk the egg yolks with the sugar until thick and creamy and then stir in the melted chocolate and the cocoa powder. Whisk the egg whites until stiff and fold them into the chocolate mixture. Pour into the prepared tin, smooth over and cook for 10 – 15 minutes or until lightly cooked. Remove from the oven and leave to cool.

Meanwhile, make the filling. Put the lemon juice and rind, the orange rind and the caster sugar into a bowl and stir until the sugar has dissolved. Add the brandy and wine. Whisk the cream in a large bowl until it is just holding its shape then whisk in a little of the lemon mixture at a time, being careful not to over-whisk, until all the liquid has been absorbed. Chill the mixture in the refrigerator.

To make the roulade, dust a piece of greaseproof paper with the icing sugar and tip the cooked chocolate mixture onto it. Spread the lemon cream all over the surface, taking it right to the edges. Holding the long ends of the chocolate base, roll it up fairly tightly like a Swiss roll, removing the paper as you roll. Then, using both hands, lift it onto a serving dish. Chill until ready to serve.

Freezer friendly — chocolate base only

Apple Tansy

SERVES 4

This is a great favourite of mine and it certainly had a nursery feel to it until I added a handful of ground almonds and a slurp of calvados. Now it is a very good pick-me-up when suffering from a cold. When I was testing this recipe, the phone rang and I burnt the apple. I carried on and the result was a caramelized apple dish, more like a tarte tatin purée. Delicious — have a go.

450g (1lb) cooking apples, peeled, cored and sliced
1 strip of lemon rind studded with 4 cloves
50g (2oz) butter
120g (4oz) caster sugar

2 eggs, separated
1 tbsp ground almonds
1 tbsp calvados
150ml (¼ pint) double cream, whipped

Put the apples, the clove-studded lemon rind, the butter and half the sugar into a heavy-based saucepan and cook over a very low heat until the apple is soft. Add a splash of water if the apple starts to stick or brown, or you can allow it to brown but watch it carefully. Remove the studded lemon rind and discard. Put the apple mixture into a blender and purée. Cool and then add the egg yolks, ground almonds, calvados and fold in the whipped cream. Whisk the egg whites until stiff and, using a metal spoon, fold them into the apple. Spoon into large glasses or a serving dish. Chill until ready to serve.

English Trifle with Strawsberries and Mango

SERVES 6

I specify a lemon cake in the recipe here but this trifle can be altered by using chocolate cake, fresh oranges and orange liqueur, coffee cake with fresh raspberries and oranges with amaretto liqueur and so on! Basically anything in the cake tin and the drinks cupboard could make a good combination.

600ml (1 pint) milk
Few drops vanilla essence
4 egg yolks
50g (2oz) caster sugar
350g (12oz) lemon sponge cake (a four-
    egg cake mixture if making it at home)

225g (8oz) strawberries, hulled and halved
1 mango, peeled, stone removed and sliced
3 tbsp cooking brandy
150ml (¼ pint) medium sherry
300ml (½ pint) double cream, whipped
Strawberries, halved, to decorate

Heat the milk and vanilla essence in a saucepan over a low heat. Beat the egg yolks and sugar together in a large bowl. When the milk is near to boiling point, whisk it into the hot milk. Pour the custard mixture back into the saucepan and then stir over a low heat until it thickens. Leave to cool.

Break up the sponge cake and layer in a serving dish with the fruit. Splash on all the alcohol and then cover with the custard. Leave to cool and top with the whipped cream. Decorate with the strawberries and chill until ready to serve.

Baked Rice Pudding

SERVES 4

Well, you either love it or hate it. Luckily for me it's the best, so at boarding school I ate all the unwanted portions! Serve with strawberry jam and whipped cream, if you wish.

50g (2oz) pudding rice
600ml (1 pint) full-fat milk

25g (1oz) caster sugar
Freshly grated nutmeg

Preheat the oven to 150°C (300°F, Gas 2). Put the rice into a ¼ litre (1½ pint) ovenproof dish and add the milk and sugar. Stir well then grate on the nutmeg. Cook in the oven for about 2 hours, stirring once after 30 minutes. Serve hot or cold.

Treacle Tart

When asking my friends what they considered to be comfort food, this came up almost every time — so here you are. Served hot with lashings of delicious ice cream, I have to say I am bound to agree with them, although with my love of Cornwall, I think clotted cream is best. To weigh the golden syrup, put the tin on the scales and deduct the weight of syrup required in the recipe.

225g (8oz) plain flour
1/2 tsp salt
120g (4oz) butter
1 egg yolk
Water, to mix

400g (14oz) golden syrup
350g (12oz) fine white breadcrumbs
2 pieces stem ginger, chopped finely, plus
    some syrup from jar – optional
Pecan nuts, roughly chopped – optional

Preheat the oven to 200°C (400°F, Gas 6). Put the flour and salt into a bowl and rub in the butter, using your fingertips, until the mixture resembles breadcrumbs.

Mix in the egg yolk with a round-bladed knife then gradually add just enough water to make the dough stick together. Knead well then roll out on a floured surface to a circle about 3mm (⅛ in) thick and wide enough to line a 20cm (8in) tart tin. Line the tin with the pastry then prick it all over with a fork.

Warm the golden syrup in a large saucepan, add the breadcrumbs, chopped ginger and, if using, 1 tbsp of syrup from the jar and the chopped pecans. Stir well then pour the mixture into the pastry case. Smooth the top and bake for 30 minutes or until slightly browned.

Freezer friendly

Summer Pudding

SERVES 4

One of the main tricks to get this perfect is to soak the bread in the juice before lining the dish so you can guarantee that the pudding will be completely red when turned out. Fresh red fruit is definitely the best for this recipe but frozen mixed red fruit is nearly as good. Don't try to make it with tinned fruit as it will turn out far too sweet. My favourite treat is to serve summer pudding with an orange muscat sweet wine.

900g (2lbs) mixed red fruit such as
strawberries, blackberries, blackcurrants
and raspberries, trimmed

120g (4oz) caster sugar
6 – 8 large slices white bread, crusts
removed

Cook the fruit with the sugar over a low heat for about 15 minutes or until soft and juicy. Leave to cool. Dip all but one of the slices of bread into the juices and use them to line a 850ml (1½ pint) pudding basin, making sure that the slices overlap slightly. Pack in the fruit adding enough juice to keep the mixture well moistened. Soak the final piece of bread in the juice and use it to cover the top of the basin. Press firmly and cover the basin with cling film. Leave for about 12 hours. To serve, remove the cling film, ease round the edge of the pudding with a palette knife and turn it out on to a serving plate. Eat the pudding fairly soon, before it loses its shape.

Freezer friendly

Honeycomb Mould

SERVES **6**

---

*This is an original 1750s recipe but if you want to spice it up a little,
add a spoonful of runny honey, a little fresh grated nutmeg and a
splash of West Country mead or brandy. To serve at a dinner party,
make in single portion moulds and serve on a tablespoon of sieved
raspberry or blackberry purée.*

600ml (1 pint) full-fat milk
3 eggs, separated
50g (2oz) caster sugar

Few drops vanilla essence
1 desp gelatine
2 tbsp water

Put the milk into a saucepan and bring it to the boil. Put the egg yolks and caster sugar into a bowl and pour on the milk, whisking continuously. Pour the mixture back into the saucepan and whisk over a low heat for a few minutes. Add the vanilla essence. Soak the gelatine in the water for a few minutes, heat it gently until runny and then stir it into the milk mixture. Leave to cool for 15 minutes. Whisk the egg whites until very stiff and fold them into the cool custard. Pour into a glass bowl or a mould and leave to set in the fridge. Turn out when ready to eat.

Claret Jelly

SERVES 6 - 8

One of the smoothest, cleanest-tasting puddings imaginable. It is very good served with fresh fruit and crème fraîche, a combination that turns it into a very smart dinner-party stunner. You can now buy many mixed fruit juices in cartons, so try your own concoctions.

425ml (¾ pint) apple juice and mango mix
50g (2 oz) caster sugar
300 ml (½ pint) red wine

4 tbsp port
4 tbsp water
3 desp gelatine

Heat the apple juice in a saucepan with the sugar until the sugar has dissolved. Add the red wine and port and stir gently. Pour the water into a small saucepan and sprinkle on the gelatine. Leave to soak for 1 minute and then dissolve over a very low heat until clear and runny but not bubbling. Pour the gelatine into the wine mixture, stir and then tip into a 1.2 litre (2 pint) jelly mould. Chill until set. To turn out, dunk the mould into a bowl of hot water for a few seconds then turn out onto a serving dish.

Lemon Pudding with Blackberry Sauce

SERVES 4

As a child I was always fascinated by how this mixture splits into two layers, giving the sponge a wonderful hidden lemon sauce. For extra indulgence, serve the pudding with blackberry sauce. The contrast of colour is superb and the flavours marry to perfection.

120g (4oz) caster sugar
50g (2oz) butter
1 tbsp boiling water
Juice and grated rind of 1 lemon
50g (2oz) plain flour
2 eggs, separated
225ml (8floz) full-fat milk

For the sauce:
225g (8oz) blackberries, fresh or frozen
50g (2oz) icing sugar

Preheat the oven to 170°C (325°F, Gas 3). Cream the sugar, butter and water in a large bowl until light and fluffy. Beat in the lemon juice and rind. Stir in the flour then the egg yolks and milk and continue beating until creamy. Whisk the egg whites until stiff and fold them into the mixture.

Pour into a greased 1 litre (1¾ pint) ovenproof dish and stand in a roasting tin. Half-fill the roasting tin with hot water and cook for about 40 minutes or until light golden.

To make the sauce, put the blackberries and icing sugar into a heavy-based saucepan. Gently cook over a very low heat, adding a little water if necessary. When soft and juicy, leave to cool. Put through a sieve and serve in a jug alongside the lemon pudding.

Freezer friendly

Plums on Toast

SERVES **4**

With my sweet tooth, I think this can make a good main course although obviously it is meant to be a pudding! Plums, unless they are very ripe, are best cooked as the flavour seems to intensify in a sweetened syrup.

450g (1lb) plums, halved and stone
  removed
85g (3oz) soft brown sugar
Juice of ½ lemon
¼ tsp cinnamon powder or 1 small
  cinnamon stick

150g (¼ pint) milk
1 egg
25g (1oz) caster sugar
Few drops vanilla essence
4 slices thick white bread, crusts removed
50g (2oz) butter

Put the plums, brown sugar, lemon juice and cinnamon into a heavy-based pan with a splash of water, cover and simmer gently for about 5 minutes or until just cooked. Put the milk, egg, caster sugar and vanilla into a shallow bowl and whisk well. Soak each slice of bread in the egg mixture. Melt the butter in a large frying pan and fry each slice of bread until golden on each side. Place the bread on a serving plate, top with the warm plums and serve.

Banoffi Pie

SERVES 6

I believe this pudding was originally made at the Hungry Monk in Sussex but now it has become a nationwide favourite. Remember that the condensed milk has to cook for 4 hours. This can be done weeks ahead, so I often boil up a few tins and then store them in the cupboard ready for a then quick pudding.

1 tin condensed milk,
85g (3oz) butter
200g (7oz) packet ginger biscuits, finely
   crushed

2 bananas
300ml (½ pint) double cream, whipped
25g (1oz) dark chocolate, grated

Put the unopened tin of condensed milk in a saucepan and then half-fill the pan with hot water. Boil for four hours, topping up the water when necessary, then leave to cool (or cool and store at this point if you wish).

Melt the butter, add the ginger biscuit crumbs and mix well. Press the mixture firmly into a 20cm (8in) cake tin or pie dish to make a base. Open the tin of condensed milk, which will now be brown, and spread it over the biscuit base.

Peel the bananas, cut them into slices and arrange them over the caramel. Top with the whipped cream and sprinkle with the grated chocolate. Chill until ready to serve.

Strawberries with Uncooked Cheesecake

SERVES 8

I came upon this idea while licking out the cheesecake bowl before attempting to wash it up. The fact that an uncooked sponge cake mixture tastes better than the cooked cake applies to cheesecake too.

900g (2lbs) ripe strawberries, hulled and halved
1 tbsp rum, Cointreau or amaretto – optional
255g (9oz) cream cheese

200g (7oz) caster sugar
½ tsp vanilla essence
1 egg
150ml (¼ pint) double cream, whipped to form soft peaks

Put the strawberries into a bowl with the liqueur, toss a few times then leave to marinate. Place all the remaining ingredients, except the cream, in a mixing bowl and beat until smooth. Fold in the whipped cream then pour the mixture into a serving dish and chill until ready to serve with the strawberries.

Sweet Snacks

Fried Ginger

A little extra garnish that can add magic to many a dish. Serve on top of duck, with ice cream or sprinkled over stewed fruit. Try it.

1 piece ginger root, peeled and cut into matchsticks

1 tbsp flour
Oil for deep frying

Toss the ginger sticks in flour to coat. Heat a little oil in a small heavy-based saucepan until very hot then fry the ginger until crisp.

Remove with a slotted spoon and drain on kitchen paper.

Sticky Hedgehog Cake

MAKES ABOUT **30** SQUARES

I was a little suspicious of this cake at first as usually I am not a great fan of dates, but after eating two pieces I was completely won over.

2 dessert apples, peeled, cored and finely
  diced
120g (4oz) sticky dates, stones removed
  and chopped
75g (3oz) dried apricots, roughly chopped
1 tsp bicarbonate of soda
225 ml (8floz) boiling water
120 g (4oz) butter
200g (7oz) caster sugar
1 egg

1 tsp vanilla essence
225g (8oz) plain flour
11/2 tsp salt

For the topping:
75g (3oz) soft dark brown sugar
50g (2oz) butter
175g (6oz) desiccated coconut
225 ml (8floz) milk

Preheat the oven to 180°C (350°F, Gas 4) and line a 30 x 35cm (12 x 14in) deep-sided baking tin with greaseproof paper. Put the fruit and bicarbonate of soda in a bowl and add the boiling water. Stir and set aside for 10 minutes.

Cream the butter and sugar until light and fluffy then add the egg, vanilla, flour and salt. Beat well. Stir in the fruit mixture and pour into the prepared tin. Smooth over and bake for about 45 minutes.

Put the brown sugar and butter into a saucepan and melt gently. Stir in the coconut and milk. Pour over the top of the cooked cake and bake for a further 20 minutes. Cool in the tin and cut into squares to serve.

Freezer friendly

The Ultimate Brownie

MAKES ABOUT 30 SQUARES

If anyone one comes up with a better Brownie than this please challenge me! When I started writing this book, Zoë, my number one cook, put a plate by my desk with small squares of this brownie and slices of fresh banana on cocktail sticks. It was breakfast time, so I presumed the treat would last all day... the plate was empty in an hour!

175g (6oz) butter
310g (11oz) dark chocolate,
1 desp cocoa powder
5 eggs
550g (1¼ lbs) caster sugar

200g (7oz) self-raising flour
125g (4oz) pecan nuts, roughly chopped
125g (4oz) fresh cherries, stones removed,
 halved and soaked in 1 tbsp rum
 overnight – optional

Preheat the oven to 180°C (350°F, Gas 4) and line a 30 x 35cm (12 x 14in) deep-sided baking tin with greaseproof paper. Melt the butter, chocolate and cocoa together in a microwave or in a saucepan over a very low heat.

Beat the eggs and sugar until thick and creamy then add the chocolate mixture. Fold in the flour, nuts and cherries, if using, and mix well. Pour into the prepared tin and smooth over. Bake in the oven for about 40 minutes, but remove well before it is cooked through as brownies are best when undercooked. Trust me.

Peanut and Chocolate Snackets

MAKES ABOUT **30** SQUARES

The first thing I do when I set foot in America is buy a packet of Reese's Peeses, one of my favourite comfort foods. Here is my own version for when I am at home in England. The originals are made with milk chocolate but I prefer plain, so the choice is yours.

200g (7oz) soft dark brown sugar
450g (1 lb) icing sugar
140g (5oz) butter, softened

560g (1¼lb) smooth peanut butter
450g (1 lb) plain or milk chocolate
50g (2oz) butter, extra

Line a 30 x 35cm (12 x 14in) baking tin with greaseproof paper. Put the brown sugar, icing sugar, 140g (5oz) butter and the peanut butter into a large bowl and beat well. Pour into the prepared tin and press down firmly. Roll the top with a rolling pin if possible, or a milk bottle, if it fits better in the tin.

Melt the chocolate with the extra 50g (2oz) butter in the microwave or in a small saucepan over a very low heat and stir well. Pour and smooth the mixture over the peanut base and leave to set in a cool place. Cut into small squares and store in an airtight container in the fridge for up to three weeks.

Nutty Banana Bread

_____

'Sticky, moist, dense and loaded with bananas', is the best way to describe this loaf. Spreading it with butter just puts the 'icing on the cake'.

450g (12oz) self-raising flour
2 heaped tsp baking powder
¼ tsp salt
50g (2oz) butter, softened

225g (8oz) sugar
2 eggs
3 very ripe bananas, peeled and mashed
125g (4oz) pecans, roughly chopped

Preheat the oven to 180C (350F, Gas 4). Line a 600ml (1 pint) loaf tin with greaseproof paper. Put the flour, baking powder and salt into a large bowl and mix well. In another bowl, beat the butter and sugar until light and fluffy. Add the eggs and continue beating. Add the rest of the ingredients, stir well and pour the mixture into the loaf tin. Smooth over the top and bake for about 1 hour or until cooked. Check by spearing the loaf with a skewer — it should come out clean. Serve warm or cold and remember the butter.

Freezer friendly

Scones with Clotted Cream and Strawberry Jam

MAKES 12 - 14

With my love of Cornwall, I suppose this has to be among my top ten favourite comfort foods. It reminds me of sitting in the garden of the Helford tea rooms with the river snaking its way past. The only advantage of eating it in my own home is the absence of a million wasps trying to hop into every piece of scone destined for my mouth. With so many good jam makers in this country, I recommend buying a good quality brand from any specialist shop. You should also make the effort to find proper clotted cream.

350g (12oz) plain flour
2 tsp baking powder
Salt

1 desp caster sugar – optional
85g (3oz) butter
7 tbsp cold milk

Preheat the oven to 220°C (425°F, Gas 7). Put the flour, baking powder, salt and sugar into a bowl and mix well. Rub in the butter with your fingertips until it resembles fine breadcrumbs. Make a well in the centre, pour in the milk and mix to a spongy dough with a round-bladed knife. Knead very lightly on a floured surface and then gently roll out to 2.5cm (1in) thick. Cut small rounds with a pastry cutter and place them gently on a baking tray. Dust with a little flour and bake for 10 minutes or until well risen and light golden brown. Serve with lashings of clotted cream and strawberry jam.

Crispy Nibbles

MAKES APPROX. 30 RIBBONS

These snackets can be picked at with a cup of coffee, served with a syllabub-type pudding, dipped in a sweet wine or just nibbled throughout a bad day. If you have any leftover fresh spaghetti, fry it up as well and toss it in the icing mix — another great nibble.

120g (4oz) self-raising flour
Caster sugar to taste
Ground cinnamon to taste
1 egg

Water, to mix
Oil for deep-frying
To dust: 25g (1oz) icing sugar mixed with
1 tsp ground cinnamon

Put the flour into a bowl with the caster sugar and cinnamon. Add the egg and mix well, adding a little water to bind, and knead into a smooth dough.

Put the dough on a floured surface and roll it out thinly. Cut into biscuit-sized strips, circles or shapes with a cutter. Heat the oil in a deep-fryer or large saucepan to 180°C (350°F) and fry a few at a time until golden brown. They should sizzle and take about 1 minute for each batch. Remove with a slotted spoon, drain on kitchen paper then toss them in the icing sugar and cinnamon mixture using a small plastic bag. Eat fresh.

Comfort Drinks

Whisky Toddy

SERVES 1

This is especially good to help clear a head cold. Make it at bedtime and, if you have a temperature, stir in a Disprin — things will be a lot better in the morning. Even without a cold, this drink is still very good and comforting.

Juice of 1 lemon
1 tsp runny honey

1 tot whisky

Put the lemon juice, honey and whisky into a cup. Pour in boiling water to fill the cup. Stir well and drink hot.

Hot Chocolate

SERVES 1

Almost everyone I consulted on comfort food has mentioned hot chocolate, so this recipe is a must!

1 mug milk
50g (2oz) dark chocolate

1 tot Baileys Irish Cream or Grand Marnier
– optional

Put the milk and chocolate into a saucepan and slowly heat to near boiling point, stirring well until the chocolate is melted. Whizz in a liquidizer, if you want a frothy drink, then add the booze and pour into a heatproof mug or glass.

Pimm's Champagne

SERVES **6** GLASSES

The best treat of the lot: a hot summer day, fresh strawberries and
mint, and a glass of Pimm's — no lemonade or tonic
— just champagne.

6 strawberries
6 leaves fresh mint
6 slices cucumber
1 peach, peeled, stone removed and cut
  into 6 slices

3 slices lime, halved
½ bottle Pimm's
1 bottle champagne, chilled

Put the strawberries, mint, cucumber, peach, lime and Pimm's into a large jug, cover and marinate for 30 minutes (if you can wait).

Slowly pour in the chilled champagne, stir and serve.

Fruit Cup

SERVES 2

For anyone on a diet, this is a very good lunchtime filler and, of course, it is very healthy for everyone else too.

1 mango, peeled, stone removed and
  roughly chopped
1 banana, peeled and sliced

6 sweet ripe strawberries, hulled
300 ml (½ pint) apple juice, chilled

Put all the ingredients into a liquidizer and whizz on high for 30 seconds or until smooth and frothy. Pour into glasses and drink.

Mulled Wine

MAKES 4 CUPS

This is perfect for Bonfire Night, when you have a few friends round on a wintry evening, or when there's just two of you escaping into a mulled wine blur.

Juice and grated rind of 1 lemon, pith and
* peel reserved*
6 cloves
15cm (6in) cinnamon stick

Juice of 2 oranges
120g (4oz) white sugar
Good splash of dark rum
1 bottle red wine

Put the juice and grated rind of the lemon into a saucepan then stud one half of the remaining lemon peel with the cloves and add it to the pan. Discard the other half. Add the cinnamon stick, orange juice, sugar and rum to the pan and heat slowly. When hot, remove from the heat, cover and leave to stand for 30 minutes. Add the red wine, reheat, strain and serve hot.

Index

INDEX